EXPERIENCING FULLNESS OF JOY IN YOUR MARRIAGE

A Dozen Roses from God

BOB UNVERZAGT

WinePressPublishing
Great Books, Defined.

WinePress Publishing (PO Box 428, Enumclaw, WA 98022) functions only as book publisher. As such, the ultimate design, content, editorial accuracy, and views expressed or implied in this work are those of the author.

ISBN 13: 978-1-60615-065-8
ISBN 10: 1-60615-065-0
Library of Congress Catalog Card Number: 2010930781

This book is dedicated to my warm and treasured wife
Joanne
with whom I am still enjoying the God-given gift
of a joyous and exciting marriage journey,
and
to our loving daughter
Sandy
already Home,
her hope in Christ realized.
She and I will dance once again
as on her wedding day.

CONTENTS

ACKNOWLEDGMENTS

From the moment I completed the first chapter, I have appealed to close friends, English majors, and professional critics for their honest feedback. Sincere compliments are always a joy, but I have requested their candid critique, and that has strengthened this Christian work. Those invited to help have frequently been couples who have strong and joyous marriages as well as familiarity with the Scriptures.

Our dear friends Ann and Wayne Whiteside have stayed very close to this project from day one, and have talked with us through pivotal and sensitive issues, sharing our same faith in Christ. They are always our faithful prayer partners. Bob Blizzard has shared his creative ideas freely, and I am indebted to him for recommending an additional short section to introduce each chapter theme with a story from our own marriage to help the reader know me as a person and as a husband. Berta Lou Dietz, my very perceptive cousin in Anchorage, Alaska, gave me many insightful comments and much warm encouragement, increasing my joy for writing.

Others who have given generously of their time and who have improved immeasurably the content and coherence of the manuscript are: Wilson ("Brad") Bradburn (English major); "Blondie" Ferguson; Pete and Doris Feil; Helen George (English teacher);

Howard and Laura Hamann; Jeanne Johnson; Tom and Nancy Kitzmiller (dearest of friends who have held as much interest in this book as Joanne and I); Nancy Kraybill; Bill and Reenie Rickard; Phil and Lisa Rudisill, our youngest reviewing couple (with four boys—three being triplets), are charting a wonderful, glowing marriage; Bill and Gail Simons; Terry and Barbara Stephens (I'll never forget their first warm response, our very first feedback left on our answering machine); Lynn Waldman of Aurora, Illinois, (professional editing); Burr and Alice Williamson; Dave and Jeanne Woo; and the encouraging and competent staff at WinePress Publishing Group in the state of Washington for their exciting concept of partnering with their authors, their aim for excellence, and their thoroughness with editing, formatting, and design.

Finally, *A Dozen Roses from God* has an appealing touch as a result of including twelve roses shot at Hershey Gardens by my nephew Eric White of Bel Air, Maryland, who has twenty-five years of experience in the graphic arts, computer technology, and digital photography; and by my niece, Cindy Bond, who has a passion for nature, an intuitive eye, and a hard-working camera!

As one who is alternately dazzled and miffed by computers, I have been most grateful for the technical support of Tom and Nancy Kitzmiller, friends who gave us their computer and helped us to get comfortable with the world of word processing; my niece, Cindy Bond, who helped me with query letters to publishers; Dave White, the son I've always wanted and now have, for his incredible speed with such things as formatting and section breaks; Jim Fairbank, my wife's brother, but also a brother to me, who more than once good-humoredly and patiently walked me through a serious snag and ultimately resolved some dark mystery; Terry Stephens, who taught me how to boldly experiment with this electronic tool without being intimidated; and especially my wife, Joanne, who did most of the word processing to allow me to write the manuscript in longhand (as I preferred) until I could learn to formulate my thoughts while working on the computer.

I am most grateful for our granddaughters, Charis and Sydney, who often have insights that seem to be beyond their years. Just as

Jesus occasionally had a child stand with him before a crowd to point out their humility and transparency, so too I find in our grandchildren rich insights and the gift of discovery.

Most important of all, I am—along with millions of others like me—profoundly influenced by the Scriptures, given to us as God's gracious and essential gift for life. No one in the entire world desires that our marriages be more joyous and hope-filled than God does! Marriage is intended by God to be the strongest of all human relationships, a secure and protected place where we can learn to love one another more deeply. If that is so, we will harvest happiness only as we listen to our Creator and learn from the Word he has so freely offered to us. That extraordinary Word comes to us in two expressions: first, as incarnated in Jesus Christ; and second, as inscribed in the written Word. The concepts in the following chapters are therefore ultimately God's gifts, and not mine.

"If I show you a rose,
you will not doubt God anymore."
—Tertullian

CHAPTER ONE

I praise you because I am fearfully and wonderfully made; your works are wonderful, I know that full well.

—Ps. 139:14

You Are Awesome!

Interpersonal

It amazes me that God trusts us so much that he allows us to participate intimately in the actual creation of a human being—a living soul! A woman understands this more than a man because the new life is formed inside her over a period of about 250 days. During the first ninety days, the incubation of this life within the warmth of the woman's protective womb is somewhat subtle. But the sense of wonder quickly escalates through the second and third trimesters of her pregnancy when she can feel the weight of the baby and actually feel the "fetus" turning over or repositioning himself/herself in some way, perhaps simply to feel more comfortable, or to enjoy a primitive "workout" by exploring some different movements. And, of course, the process of giving birth—despite its long hours of acute pain, desperate struggle, exhausting work, and sweat and tears—is for most women an experience in wonder that is virtually miraculous and sacred—an experience that even the most sensitive father cannot quite fathom as a mother does. Nevertheless, fathers who take the time to enjoy the development of their tiny offspring have their own stories about the wonder of this new life with tiny fingers and toes.

During the first few months of our daughter's infancy, Joanne and I would often stand beside her crib and just enjoy watching

1

her yawn, or see her face scrunched up for a few seconds, perhaps due to some discomfort or pain in her tummy. One day as we were standing near Sandy in her infant seat, we saw a most significant moment in her development. She was in the process of discovering her right hand. As her hand moved, she caught sight of the movement directly in front of her face and stared at her hand as she might later examine a rattle or toy. She turned it this way and that for an unhurried observation.

She was so fascinated with her discovery that she scarcely knew we were there only twelve to fifteen inches from her hand. Almost in a whisper, my wife said softly, not wanting to break Sandy's concentration, "She's discovering her hand for the first time!" Sandy's face showed delight in what she saw and while she would not take her eyes off this splendid hand—which would turn out to be her own hand—her legs gave a couple of quick kicks in the air as a result of her excitement.

After we had enjoyed this moment, I took her other hand, which was by her side and out of sight, and said to her teasingly, "Hey, look here! If you think that is special, you have another one on this side that also belongs to you!" Almost without taking her eyes off her hand above her, and without so much as a glance at me even for a second, she quickly took her left hand and thrust it down against her side where it had been before. We both smiled and my wife concluded, "We understand, it's a lot to take in. When you discover that you have a wonderful hand attached to you, you're just not ready for the whole idea of having two!"

INSPIRING

> Then God said, "Let us make man in our image, in our likeness, and let them rule over the fish of the sea and the birds of the air, over the livestock, over all the earth, and over all the creatures that move along the ground." So God created man in his own image, in the image of God he created him; male and female he created them. God blessed them and said to them, "Be fruitful and increase in number; fill the earth and subdue it. Rule over

the fish of the sea and the birds of the air and over every living creature that moves on the ground."

—Gen. 1:26–28

When I consider your heavens, the work of your fingers, the moon and the stars, which you have set in place, what is man that you are mindful of him, the son of man that you care for him? You made him a little lower than the heavenly beings and crowned him with glory and honor. You made him ruler over the works of your hands; you put everything under his feet: all flocks and herds, and the beasts of the field, the birds of the air, and the fish of the sea, all that swim the paths of the seas. O LORD our Lord, how majestic is your name in all the earth!

—Ps. 8:3–9

Don't you know that you yourselves are God's temple and that God's Spirit lives in you? . . . for God's temple is sacred, and you are that temple.

—1 Cor. 3:16–17

IMAGINING

Moments of Creation

Light explodes the darkness in its first year's headlong run!
Wild, whirling fire is tamed
To gently kiss the earth.
Planets are customized by God—
One with furious, freezing, unceasing hurricane winds;
Another with a bloated, boiling surface;
Yet another adorned with a breathtaking ice-crystal necklace
Of many cosmic strands—
All then jettisoned into smooth silent orbs of inky nothingness!
And God was pleased!
With the Creator's infinite power,
Stars infinite in number
Are flung out into a sea of infinite space,
Along with countless galaxies
Identified by their signature shapes of gaseous hues—
With ten million years to wait the quasar's debut.
The oceans fill at his nod,

To heave and roll till the end of time.
Breakers–empowered until they crest in creamy foam—
Checked by God for their timeless beauty
In a millionth of a second—
The fractured water then ordained to everlasting motion!
Mountains extravagantly pile up with a deafening grating.
Wounds of bleeding lava seep through steaming crevices.
Rivers chew their first terrestrial path to open seas.
Hurricane and tidal wave and earthquake are unleashed,
Letting us behold the tiniest fraction of his power!
Then, ever changing cloud formations march across his skies.
Spectacles of color in morning's stunning sunrise:
Crimson reds, fiery oranges, and passionate magentas
Wildly streaming
And a myriad of flowers,
Each of exquisite design,
Require a pallet of incalculable hues.
And then a day for details—
Lumbering elephants and breaching whales,
Whiskered seals and centipedes,
Neon fish and multi-dexterous octopi,
Cheetah and mosquito, fox and ox, wasp and wren,
Antelopes attentive,
And stately flamingos aflame with vivid pink
And in a lighter moment,
Sand crabs to walk sprightly sideways!
Then smilingly the Creator dreams up a bulldog's face!
Ten million species in all,
Formed by his untiring mind,
Not a single species endangered.
With time left to create the elegance of snowfall,
The restorative rain,
The whistling wind,
The mesmerizing fire!
But his consummate, climactic, and crowning work,
Wondrously fashioned from a gob of earth
And a bit of rib,
Was man and woman—
Fearfully and wondrously wrought!

INTERPRETING

The most significant thing that can be said about *you* is that you were designed by God's creative mind! You did not happen accidentally. You were made purposefully and thoughtfully by the greatest intelligence in the universe—the only *infinite* intelligence in the universe. Because of this one single fact, no man or woman living on this planet should ever have to experience a diminished self-esteem. You and I were made just "a little lower than the heavenly beings" (Ps. 8:5).

Whenever I read the magnificent creation account in Genesis, the words stir me. Perhaps because I instinctively sense a linkage with Adam and Eve. And just as they were created by a decisive act of God, I believe God by his infinite power created you and me.

This awesome understanding about our identity and origin is mind-boggling to say the least. It is such a grand thought that it nearly borders on the inconceivable, the unfathomable, the unimaginable! Perhaps that is why the simplicity of Anne B. Snow's hymn, "Wherever I May Wander," is so helpful. It gathers up all the wonder of this Christian belief and renders it thinkable:

> Wherever I may wander,
> Wherever I may be,
> I am certain of my Maker's love;
> God's care is over me.
> God made the great high mountains,
> And made the wide blue sea;
> God made the sky where airplanes fly;
> God made the world, and me![1]

Some time back, our daughter's family visited us for the weekend. While I was cleaning the kitchen after our family breakfast, I heard my son-in-law, Dave, doing a spontaneous "teaching moment" with his seven-year-old twin daughters, Charis and Syd. Somehow *the hand* had become the subject of conversation and Dave saw in it an opportunity to teach them something very special. He said something like this. "Girls, did you know that your hands have been made by God in such a wonderful way that there is nothing in all the world that can do as many different things as your hands? Just think about it. You can climb a tree, throw or catch a ball—well, most of the time! You can do a watercolor with Pop-Pop or help Grandma pull weeds in her flowerbeds. Your hand weighs less than a pound, yet you can use it to do cartwheels and somersaults, to operate a computer or cell phone, and many other things as well. There is nothing in the whole universe that is as capable and as skillful as your hands."

That observation had never occurred to me. What a marvelous design! What amazing versatility! And to think that we come equipped with not one, but two of these remarkable manipulators. Furthermore, God placed them strategically in complementary and opposing positions so they can work effectively as a team—to do such sophisticated tasks as playing a piano or harp, or piloting a cruise ship. And while Dave was explaining the hand's many uses to our granddaughters, I was thinking, *And they are very good at stacking plates in the cupboard and scrubbing pots and pans!*

What is true of your hand is also true of your eyes . . . or your heart . . . or your brain! Each of these three complex parts of your body, considered apart from the others, is wondrous in terms of its incredible functioning and sophisticated design and compactness. One might also add that the arrangement in which God has put them all together into the design of our bodies is itself sublime. That is to say, God has given us a shape that is ingenious in every detail. Our body, as the "housing" for everything else, is not only symmetrical, synchronized, and capable of an infinite number of movements and tasks through the fluidity of our muscles and the strong frame of our skeleton, but also in its totality is a remarkable harmony and oneness beautiful to behold, whether it is still or in motion. God designed you with all of these amazing features and consequently you are, as the psalmist observed thousands of years ago, "fearfully and wonderfully made"!

But when we think of you, and the wonderful way God made you, all that has been said is just the beginning. You are so much more than just a rare and elaborate machine or structure designed for an infinite number of motions and activities. You are an intellectual and spiritual being that can do truly remarkable functions. For example, you can "get" an idea, such as painting a sunset with watercolors, then gather all of the appropriate materials, possibly take a class on watercolor painting, do the painting itself, and afterwards look at it reflectively to critique it, appreciate it, or simply enjoy it suitably framed for your home. Or you can walk into a bookstore that offers thousands of books on countless subjects, and after browsing you can select several books that you really want to read, and know why you have chosen those books from among the thousands available. You are able to think through complex situations by reasoning, do problem solving, and make choices after examining many possible options to arrive at the best results. Your mind is able to process rather simple projects, such as planning how you will landscape your new home, to extremely sophisticated and complex processes, such as designing and engineering a 500-passenger cruise ship.

You are also an emotional being capable of laughter and tears. Your face, made up of an amazing mosaic of muscles (forty-two, to be precise), is capable of non-verbally communicating disdain, delight, disappointment, sadness, surprise, sympathy, anger, approval, astonishment, fear, flirtation, frustration, and hundreds of other emotions as well. You are a being who can mentally "stand outside yourself" and consider yourself as though you were not a part of yourself. You are able to think in three dimensions—past, present, and future.

And most amazing of all your capacities (which are so numerable that what we have talked about here is merely suggestive—the tip of the iceberg—at best) you are intermingled and integrated with a spirit that allows you not only to contemplate God, but also to communicate or commune with him! This is possible because God has made us as both material bodies and as spiritual beings, each one mysteriously superimposed upon the other to form an integrated unity, which we normally call a *person*. And so, the apostle Paul writes to his friends in Corinth some twenty centuries ago, "Don't you know that you yourselves are God's temple and that God's Spirit *lives in you*? . . . for God's temple is sacred, and *you are that temple*" (1 Cor. 3:16–17, emphasis mine).

By now you may be wondering what all this has to do with a book on marriage. For now, it is sufficient to say, there is a strong human inclination to miss the wonder all around us and to take the most amazing features of our lives in a ho-hum fashion. In Proverbs 30:18–19 the writer names four things that are "too amazing" for him to take in, the fourth being "the way of a man with a maiden." I am not sure what amazed him specifically about that relationship—perhaps the excitement and attraction that takes place in flirtation and courtship, the astonishing depth of commitment and caring that forges a strong and lasting marriage, the ecstasy of being held and touched as lovers become one in the fullness of intercourse, perhaps any or all of these.

What I do know is that the writer was in touch with the wonder of what he was experiencing with a woman. My hope is this. As we think about marriage, and specifically the marriage we are in, are we aware of how much God has creatively invested in the whole concept of marriage and intimacy, and how much care he has taken in designing us so that we might experience together the most sublime and satisfying experiences of giving and receiving?

I read somewhere that a teacher gave her elementary school class the assignment of compiling their own list of the Seven Wonders of the World. They came up with this very impressive list:

1. Taj Mahal
2. Panama Canal
3. Grand Canyon
4. Pyramids
5. St. Peter's Basilica
6. Great Wall of China
7. Empire State Building

The class seemed pleased with the list except one little girl. The teacher asked if she needed help. She told the teacher that she was having trouble picking only seven. The teacher asked her to share with the class some of her choices to see if the class agreed. The girl then read from her paper:

1. Seeing
2. Hearing
3. Touching
4. Feeling
5. Laughing
6. Thinking
7. Loving

When she finished, you could have heard a pin drop in that room. Each of these capacities constitutes a significant part of the persons we are. Relatively speaking, these spiritual and emotional capacities are even more awesome than the physical structure of our bodies—awe-inspiring as that may be! No wonder the psalmist exclaims, "I praise you, for I am fearfully and wonderfully made."

The hymn, "I Was There to Hear Your Borning Cry," was written by John Ylvisaker in 1985. I find it rather challenging to sing, but the beautiful tune is worth learning, and the words are moving:

> I was there to hear your borning cry,
> I will be there when you are old,
> I rejoiced the day you were baptized,
> To see your life unfold.
>
> I was there when you were but a child,
> With a faith to suit you well;
> I will be there in case you wander off
> And find where demons dwell.
>
> When you found the wonder of the Word,
> I was there to cheer you on;
> You were raised to praise the living God,
> To whom you now belong.
>
> Should you find someone to share your time
> And you join your hearts as one,
> I will be there to make your verses rhyme
> From dusk to rising sun.
>
> In the middle ages of your life,
> Not too old, no longer young,
> I will be there to guide you through the night,
> Complete what I have begun.
>
> When the evening gently closes in
> And you shut your weary eyes,
> I will be there as I have always been
> With just one more surprise.
>
> I was there to hear your borning cry,
> I will be there when you are old.
> I rejoiced the day you were baptized,
> To see your life unfold.[2]

If you and your spouse have problems in your marriage, God has designed both of you in such a magnificent way that you have within yourselves the extraordinary means to solve your problems. As you each listen in quiet, reflective moments, God will give you his profound, personal thoughts for you both through his Spirit living within you. And even better, if you wish to *avoid* major problems throughout your marriage, you have the special blueprint of his Word to guide you day by day.

In summary, our human situation, with marriage as a notable option, could not be more hope-filled, or have more possibilities for joy and fulfillment. Saint Angela of Foligno, one of the great spiritual guides for Christian meditation who greatly admired St. Francis, once put it this way: "Our condition is most noble, being so beloved of the most-high God that he was willing to die for our sake—which he would not have done if man had not been a most noble creature and of great worth."

INTEGRATING

There is nothing in all creation that has the awesome possibilities and capabilities that you and I have! Our generous Creator has endowed us in every conceivable way. Now I need to ask an important question. What are the implications of this belief in relationship to marriage? If we believe that God exquisitely and wonderfully made us, what difference does that make in terms of a person's role as a marriage partner?

Raising the Bar of Marital Bliss

For sure, we are persons to be envied! Consider our situation for a moment. We believe God has given us his Spirit to reside within us. This allows us to have a "direct line" to God, who just happens to be the most knowledgeable Person in the universe when it comes to the subject of marriage. Equally important, he is a God of goodness who wants only the best for us. Jesus, as God's Son, once said something that must have surprised the disciples, men who understood God as the giver of the Ten Commandments:

> As the Father has loved me, so have I loved you. Now remain in my love. If you obey my commands, you will remain in my love, just as I have obeyed my Father's commands and remain in his

love. I have told you this so that my joy may be in you and that
your joy may be complete.

—John 15:9–11

The God we know through Jesus Christ is not a God who is eager
to condemn us. He wants our joy to be complete. He also wants us
to enjoy the generous gift of his forgiveness. The psalmist beautifully
proclaims the fullness of that forgiveness. "He does not treat us as
our sins deserve or repay us according to our iniquities. For as high
as the heavens are above the earth, so great is his love for those who
fear him; as far as the east is from the west, so far has he removed our
transgressions from us" (Ps. 103:10–12).

Our Father in heaven wants to give us a clean slate and set us free
from all of our guilt and fears; our self-doubt and self-disdain; and our
sarcasm, pessimism, and cynicism. He is the God of hope, not despair;
the God of light, not darkness; the God of graciousness, not grudges.
So do not think for a moment that when you seek God's will for your
marriage he is going to lecture you for any personal failings, or tell you to
expect less in your marriage, or to quickly bail out. What you can more
likely expect of God is remarkable insight and wisdom that you can
apply to your own situation, or a surprisingly hope-filled perspective on
your attitude or approach to your marriage—a view you possibly would
have never conceived or considered on your own.

As for problems, nothing is beyond God's restoration, resolution,
or re-creation. Consider for a moment a few problems God has
already solved:

1. How do you restore life to a man who has been dead for a
   few days? (For the account of the raising of Lazarus by Jesus,
   see John 11:38–44.)
2. How do you create a planet the size of Jupiter (having a
   diameter roughly eleven times the earth's diameter) and float
   it silently through space at the exhilarating speed of 25,000
   miles an hour, marking an invisible orbit so large that it will
   require more than a decade to complete just one circle—and
   then repeat that orbiting indefinitely?

11

3.   What do you do to get the serious attention, response, and long-term personal consideration of millions of people, whose inclinations are centered, for the most part, on self and pleasure?

These three problems are a part of God's resume, yet they are but a small sampling of what his power and intelligence can do. Could anyone really think that his or her marital frustrations or long-standing conflicts are beyond God's capacity or intelligence?

God will guide your marriage the moment he knows you are genuinely and humbly inviting him to provide his divine insight into your personal situation. Once we understand this, we are ready to embark on an adventure that is like no other—the restoration, renewal, and re-creation of your marriage.

Let us begin the venture!

A Prayer

Lord, I thank you for the awesome and incredible way you have created me as a person, and for the special helpmate you have given to me as my life partner. I thank you that you have so "wonderfully made" both of us, designed to be a source of joy to one another, and to you. Teach us how to place our marriage in your gracious hands so we can deepen our relationship and make it as beautiful as you had in mind for Adam and Eve in the beginning. In the name of Jesus. Amen.

Three Questions

1.   If you could take the most baffling and most frustrating part of your marriage to God for his input, what would it be?
2.   What do you suppose God would graciously say to you today about your marriage?
3.   In your spare moments during the next twenty-four hours do some creative reflection on your mate—naming those qualities you most like about her/him. (You might want to keep a small pad in your pocket or purse for recording your

thoughts.) Then share your thoughts with your spouse and/
or offer thanks to God for the person your spouse is.

INSIGHTS

The most important thing to come out of the mine is the miner.

—Frederick Le Play

What we are is God's gift to us. What we become is our gift to
God.

—Anonymous

Made in God's image, man was made to be great, he was made to
be beautiful, and he was made to be creative in life and art.

—Frances A. Schaeffer

The kingdom of God is within you.

—Luke 17:21

Christ has made my soul beautiful with the jewels of grace and
virtue.

—Saint Agnes

Miracles, in the sense of phenomena we cannot explain, surround
us on every hand: life itself is the miracle of miracles.

—George Bernard Shaw

The greatest miracle of all, the human being.

—Marya Mannes

CHAPTER TWO

If you obey my commands, you will remain in my love, just as I have obeyed my Father's commands and remain in his love. I have told you this so that my joy may be in you and that your joy may be complete.

—John 15:10–11

The One Essential of Marriage: Joy

INTERPERSONAL

Our family was extremely excited when planning for our daughter's wedding. Several months in advance she set the date for a July wedding. Joanne and I planned our summer flowers so they were all white in honor of her wedding day. We gave Sandy and her fiancé, Dave, a "budget" to give them some direction as to how much we could help them with flowers, the reception, bridal gown, wedding cake, etc. They were great about keeping in the given range.

One day Joanne and I were enjoying lunch at a resort that happened to be promoting a new wedding package that included a beautiful new chapel, limousine service, and reception options in a gracious court area featuring a spiral staircase—Sandy's dream since childhood for her wedding day. We shared all this with Sandy and Dave, and all of us were excited about the ease of making all the arrangements, the lovely atmosphere of the resort, and the idea of a single location for both the wedding service and the reception, simplifying the day for everyone. Our own church facility was too small for the number of invited guests, so that problem was also resolved.

All of the arrangements were made and the excitement kept growing. As we got closer to the wedding day, it dawned on me that when a couple marries they have eight grandparents who have greatly influenced their lives. All four of Sandy's grandparents had been very active in her life, but by this time all four were deceased. Dave's situation was similar except that one of his grandparents was still living. However, because of health problems she could not be at their wedding. I began searching for some way to honor these eight people at the wedding because they had been so influential in Sandy and Dave's lives.

The wedding already seemed to have enough frills—a stretch limousine was a stretch for a pastor's income! Nevertheless, I soon came up with the idea of having a swan ice sculpture in the center of the reception area with an artistically written placard that simply said:

In Honor of Sandy and Dave's Grandparents

It was our surprise for their wedding day. Our family had never done anything this extravagant, but it turned out to be one of the best decisions ever! I will never forget our daughter's stunned surprise and joy as she gazed from a balcony area at the reception area below and spotted the illuminated ice sculpture. Photographed by many of our guests throughout the day, it elicited many compliments and remarks. Nothing can exceed the joy of a daughter's wedding day, but this gesture of love for their grandparents was for our family an additional joyous memory.

Inspiring

> The Lord your God is with you, he is mighty to save. He will take great delight in you, he will quiet you with his love, he will rejoice over you with singing.
>
> —Zeph. 3:17

> If you obey my commands, you will remain in my love, just as I have obeyed my Father's commands and remain in his love. I have told you this so that my joy may be in you and that your joy may be complete.
>
> —John 15:10–11

Rejoice in the Lord always. I will say it again: Rejoice!

—Phil. 4:4

Imagining

The delicious feeling of joyousness comes to us through a great variety of experiences ranging from a warm hug to the more complex emotional mix of the inner satisfaction and joy of a volunteer who spends a week or two in a third world nation building modest homes for families barely surviving in makeshift shacks. As we become more aware of what brings us a profound sense of joy, we can plan our lives so that our decisions enable such joys to happen. I share below a very partial list of things that bring me joy to stimulate your thoughts about the kinds of experiences that could be a joy to you.

A Journal of Joys Randomly Remembered

- Pausing to watch the spectacle of Canada geese flying in near perfect "V" formations—their relentless honking continually encouraging their flight leaders
- Being enthusiastically greeted by my dog Skip after school—often thrown to the floor by his exuberance—his tail wildly wagging his welcome, while at the same time he licked my face
- Reaching the shelter of the barn just as a spring storm breaks into a heavy downpour
- Feeling the first muted "kick" of our baby, still being amazingly formed inside Joanne's body by our loving Creator
- Visiting a friend who has felt depressed for weeks and getting him to laugh again
- Watching the gray silhouette of a possum as he waddles across the road at dusk
- Sharing in a catch-up, end-of-the-day conversation with my wife on our screened porch, while enjoying a sultry summer breeze and a glass of iced cinnamon spice tea

- Being enthusiastically invited by our six-year-old grand-daughter, Charis, to go on her favorite roller coaster ride as the last ride of our family day
- Having a time of quiet for reflection and prayer in which I was really genuinely interested in knowing God's thoughts on a personal problem, and then receiving clear guidance and encouragement from Jesus—almost before my prayer had ended
- Driving back home around 3:00 A.M. in a deep winter snow, with a loaded pistol on the seat beside me, after spending a few hours talking a guy out of suicide, and sharing with him my knowledge of a loving God—a God who loved him as much as he loved me
- Feeling the ticklish sensation of a caterpillar's rhythmic walk over and around my extended hand
- Making it through college finals—not at all clear about what grades I would receive, but knowing in my heart I had given it my best shot
- Seeing the surprise on my wife's face when I escorted her into the Saturn showroom and told her the red car with the huge bow on its roof was her birthday gift
- Holding a newborn kitten's fragile body, gently stroking the delicate softness of her thin fur and hearing her almost inaudible purring
- Introducing a man to Jesus, and seeing his life changing perceptibly month after month, becoming a more caring, more helpful, more considerate, and more Christlike person—who in turn inspired and re-ignited my own faith out of its doldrums and into a more exciting and authentic season of growth
- Being called into the dean's office at Princeton seminary to be told confidentially that a generous alumnus—who had been apprised of my financial situation—had anonymously donated the full cost of my senior year of study as a pre-ministerial student

- Setting up a pretend hospital and appointing my grand-daughter Syd as nurse on duty and playing doctor until the broken leg of her doll was mended, and my granddaughter's tears had disappeared
- Receiving an exquisitely detailed model of the *U.S.S. Constitution*, replicating every sail, rope, and knot on the original vessel— the incredible thank you gift of a new friend who had nearly committed suicide just a month earlier
- Spontaneously inviting a married couple (visiting our church) out to dinner, and then sensing a deep friendship coming alive during the brief hours we enjoyed together
- Feeling the tiny fingers of our newborn daughter Sandy grasp my little finger with her first formed fist—accompanied by a very surprised look in her wide-open eyes upon discovering the marvelous capacity of her still-rosy hand to squeeze tightly
- Teaching our granddaughters, Charis and Syd, how to do a watercolor portrait of their favorite stuffed animal at age seven
- Sharing in the wonder and joy of unhurried cuddling and lovemaking with my wife as the perfect ending to any day

INTERPRETING

Less than twenty-four hours before his suffering and death, Jesus spent the evening having dinner with his twelve disciples. Much of what he shared with them that night he had taught them earlier. However, this particular night was Jesus' final opportunity to give them a clearer understanding of who he was and why he had come. At one point in the evening he paused to say something quite surprising, "I have told you this *so that my joy may be in you and that your joy may be complete*" (John 15:11, emphasis mine). Later that same evening, Jesus prayed for his exhausted disciples as they slept nearby, confiding in the Father what was foremost on his mind. "I am coming to you now, but I say these things while I am still in the world, *so that they may have the full measure of my joy within them*" (John 17:13, emphasis mine).

In these two passages, Jesus speaks of joy as his inexhaustible resource (like his eternal love for us) that he wants to give us as his personal gift. Isn't it intriguing that Jesus, the one who lavishes upon us so many wonderful and priceless gifts—for example, his unconditional forgiveness, his unfailing presence in our hearts, his astonishing redemption through the cross, and the staggering hope of eternal life—desires to give us yet another? It is the priceless gift of joy! At this last hour joy is the gift par excellence that he wished to bestow on us in full measure.

The subject of joy is no stranger to God's Word. The word *joy* (and its synonyms) occurs two hundred times throughout the Bible. The prophet Zephaniah speaks reassuringly to the floundering and discouraged remnant of Israel. "The LORD your God is with you, he is mighty to save. *He will take great delight in you*, he will quiet you with his love, *he will rejoice over you with singing*" (3:17, emphasis mine). God not only wants our lives to be full of joy, he also finds in us a cause for joy within himself. What possibly could be more encouraging to us? Jesus not only wants our lives to be flooded with the fullness of his own joy, but a part of his own joy originates in us—he takes great delight in us and rejoices over us.

Likewise, as we come to know God in a stronger and fuller relationship, we find joy and fulfillment in his presence with us. Consequently, the psalmist says, "Then will I go to the altar of God, *to God, my joy and my delight*" (Ps. 43:4, emphasis mine). God is our greatest blessing and our highest joy! Or consider Psalm 16:11. "You have made known to me the path of life; *you will fill me with joy in your presence, with eternal pleasures at your right hand*" (emphasis mine). God has always wanted to fill our hearts with his joy! No wonder it is Jesus' final word for his disciples!

The life of joy that is God's plan for us is emphasized repeatedly throughout the New Testament. When the apostle John writes his three epistles, he says in the prologue, "The life [of Jesus Christ] appeared; we have seen it and testify to it, and we proclaim to you the eternal life, which was with the Father and has appeared to us" (1 John 1:2). Then he writes as the ending to his introduction, and just before he begins the main body of his message, "We write this *to make our joy complete*" (1 John 1:4, emphasis mine). Knowing who

God is in the person of his Son, Jesus Christ—a God who is the source of light, love, and joy—becomes a tremendous source of joy to both the writer, John, and to his readers.

Later, in a follow-up letter directed to "the chosen lady and her children," John the apostle stresses the importance of living out God's love through a life of obedience and then concludes, "I have much to write to you, but I do not want to use paper and ink. Instead, I hope to visit you and talk with you face to face, *so that our joy may be complete*" (2 John 12, emphasis mine). Joy was the outcome of our introduction to this God who lavishes upon us his priceless gifts of a full forgiveness, a rich redemption, the power of his presence within our hearts through his Holy Spirit, and the assurance of everlasting life. Bring together a few people who believe that these promised blessings are in fact realities for them, and you create friendships that exude a contagious joy and excitement that keep drawing in others. This drawing power, which is caused by the life of Jesus Christ and his works among us, explains why the first century church grew by leaps and bounds, even during times of ruthless persecution.

When Christ commissions seventy-two disciples to go out to other towns and share what God was doing through his Son, we are afterward told by Luke that "the seventy-two returned with joy" (Luke 10:17). I would have loved to have been there to catch their excitement and to hear firsthand the stories of the people they met, how they were given opportunities to share their incredibly good news for the entire inhabited world, and ultimately, how they drew many people to Jesus Christ. I will venture a guess that the seventy-two never divided into committees before they started out. Neither did they wait until the completion of a twelve-month demographic study of the target population!

Even their considerable difficulties traveling over dusty roads—often without the advantage of horses, camels, or even donkeys—did not diminish their spirits. They still arrived home, brimming with joy and excitement. How was this possible? Their joy could not be squelched, suppressed, or silenced because they were giving to the world a beautiful portrait of God—a God of love who takes delight in each of us as the creative work of his hands. They lovingly preached about a personal God revealed through his beloved Son, Jesus Christ, who, above all else, wants us to be the glad recipients of his joy—a joy that floods our hearts and is full and complete.

One time when our granddaughters were six, we were enjoying a family gathering at our daughter's home. The topic of conversation had somehow come upon the subject of hairstyle (or, for a few of us, the lack of hair!), and my family was having some harmless fun teasing me about my obvious shortfall in this area. At the time, I was sitting Indian-style on the floor, thinking to myself that this was all going over the heads of the girls, who were playing a board game.

All of a sudden, Charis stood up and came over to me. She stood in front of me and asked, "Pop-pop, is it okay for me to touch your hair?" I had no idea what was coming, but I said, "Sure." She walked around to my right side and patted my hair so lightly I could scarcely feel her touch. Then without saying a word, she walked around to my left side and did the same thing, ever so lightly. She then returned to her original position. Because I was seated on the floor, my eyes were precisely at her level. Charis then gently took her hands and lovingly placed them on my cheeks as a parent might do when he/she wants the full attention of a child. She then announced her findings to me. "Pop-pop, *you have enough!*" I felt affirmed for weeks!

Who does not eagerly look forward to such joyous experiences in his or her life, however they might come to us? Who would refuse to pray with the psalmist, "Let me hear joy and gladness" (Ps. 51:8)? If we realize that God is by no means a killer of joy and happiness, but the very one who wants our lives to overflow with joy, would not we feel more free to be joyous people, not only for the sake of our spouses, but for every family member, friend, and work associate to whom we relate on a daily basis?

Let us come at this from a totally different perspective. Suppose for a moment that we had no scriptures to tell us of Jesus' fervent prayer for us that our joy may be complete in him. Would a dour God have made pelicans, porpoises, and pocketed kangaroos for our delight? Would Jesus, who is identified as both the creator and sustainer of the entire universe, have given us mischievous monkeys, elongated dachshunds, waddling ducks, and graceful giraffes for some other reason than to delight us? If Jesus were a gloomy, glum, or even grim personality, would he have created bullfrogs that look as if they have been involved in some mix-up and received cow's eyes? If Jesus were a dreary or dismal personality, would he have come up with a camel that looks as if he was composed of too much material and the excess had to be put somewhere? Surely, Jesus was thoroughly enjoying the process of creation when he designed yapping puppies and purring kittens for the children of his world to enjoy. Or consider the appearance of any animal during its first few days of existence. Do not they all have the ability to put a smile on your face, whether it is a newborn colt, a collie, or a chimpanzee?

How did Jesus (or God) ever get the bad rap of being severe and deadly serious when he is the one who poured from his infinite palette every color imaginable to create the breathtaking splendor of sunsets, each viewable from any vantage point on the earth, and glorious reminders of his faithful presence in our lives! Would a joyless or cheerless God have created thread-like waterfalls that cascade a quarter of a mile off towering cliffs before splashing into the peaceful, pristine fiords of Norway? Would a God who was miserly with us have created the astonishing beauty of shaded glens, glacier fields, flashing streams, towering redwoods, tropical forests, and snow-capped mountains? What was God's purpose in creating the Grand Canyon and Niagara Falls, if it were not to give us goose bumps, a feeling of wonder, and a pervasive joy? Surely God created the crashing waves on ten thousand shorelines, fully realizing they would one day become the playgrounds for children and adults alike, who together would splash and dance in their endless churning motion, surfboard on their smooth rolling power, and then try to capture their breathtaking beauty with camera or canvas. On every day that God created, he finished his work by evening and pronounced that it was "good." That is to say, he felt a sense of delight and joy in the completed canvas of creation. So, too, we should enjoy all of these things as his gifts to us—excellent, exquisite, and extraordinary gifts intended to give us fullness of joy.

Joy: One Tough Commodity!

I do not readily or normally think of joy as a quality that has toughness. For me, there is something incompatible and almost contradictory about the statement in Nehemiah 8:10: "Do not grieve, for the *joy of the LORD* is *your strength*" (emphasis mine). The context of that verse is the highly dramatic first reading of God's law in Jerusalem after the exiles return from Babylon to rebuild the city. The Law had to be read outdoors to accommodate the vast crowd of people. It was read by Ezra, "the scribe" who stood on a large platform built for this special occasion. Thirteen other officials stood with him on the platform, and every one of their names is recorded in the Bible.

The people were so moved by this sacred reading of the Law (essentially Leviticus) that they began to weep and grieve—grieving because this custom had been neglected for many years. Then Nehemiah sought to encourage them by saying, in effect, that this was not an occasion to mourn, but a time to celebrate. "Do not grieve, for the joy of the LORD is your strength" (Neh. 8:10).

Then the Scriptures say that, "the people went away to eat and drink" and "to celebrate with great joy" (Neh. 8:12). Whenever we return to the Lord, he wants to give us his joy through his presence in our lives—a joy that becomes an important part of our spiritual foundation and interior strength. God does not want us bemoaning our past failures and our years spent away from him—he wants us to celebrate today that we are at last back home, once again genuinely placing our faith and trust in him and his Word.

Jesus gave a similar teaching in his well-known parable of the prodigal son found in Luke 15:11–32. When the prodigal son finally regains his senses and returns home, his father does not say a single word about the son's foolishness or condemn him for wasting his inheritance. Instead, he immediately hugs his son and begins giving orders to the household servants about putting together a fantastic party that very day to celebrate the son's return to the family circle. If you read the parable carefully, you discover the son never really completed his carefully rehearsed apology, mainly because his father's joy and exuberance had already kicked in—an intense joy he wanted the entire household to experience.

When the apostle Paul writes from prison to the church at Philippi, he is fully aware that he could soon be put to death. Yet he says, "Even if I am being poured out like a drink offering . . . I am glad and rejoice with all of you. So too you should be glad and rejoice with me" (Phil. 2:17–18). Later, in the same short epistle, he says, "Rejoice in the Lord *always*. I will say it again: Rejoice!" (Phil. 4:4, emphasis mine). The joy referred to in the Bible can always be traced back to our Lord, and it can transform a large grieving crowd into a celebrative people of God. This biblical joy will also remain quietly steadfast with you even through the anxiety of a prison sentence. The joy referred to in the Bible is one tough commodity!

While I was serving as a pastor of a small congregation in the Philadelphia area, our church treasurer, Joe Eby, had a stroke that caused him to lose the use of his right arm. He was determined to rehabilitate his arm through aggressive physical therapy and faithful exercising, and even insisted that I continue to shake his right hand on Sundays even though he had to use his left hand to lift it up for a handshake! When all efforts had failed after several months of exercise, he began to teach himself how to write with his left hand. One of the most joyous people in that entire congregation, known for his quick wit often accompanied with a wink of the eye and a contagious laughter, Joe never once asked to be relieved of his work as church treasurer. Today he continues to serve in that office, having kept the church finances for some twenty-five years with high, professional standards. He is still a joyous person who can easily chuckle over some story or laugh at something foolish he did.[3] "The joy of the LORD is your strength" (Neh. 8:10). Therefore, "Rejoice in the Lord always. I will say it again: Rejoice!" (Phil. 4:4).

Joy in Singleness, Joy in Marriage

None of the two hundred biblical references to joy ever declare, or even imply, that joy is a quality attained only through marriage. Rather, every passage of Scripture that speaks of "joy" or "joyousness" does so in a universal sense—that is, it is a fruit of the Spirit for all creation—whether single or married. We do not have to get married to experience the joy God wants us to possess. In fact, too many people believe that if they simply marry Betsy or Ben or Connie or Craig, they will find the joy and happiness they crave. To believe such a myth is to become disillusioned with your marriage in a very short time. Any person who seeks marriage had better make sure he has dealt with his own grayness or dullness first. Ask yourself, "Why am I so often sad or irritable, cantankerous or complaining? Why am I so frequently angry or argumentative, resistant or rebellious?" If we enter marriage before resolving these bad attitudes, we simply will transfer all of these problems and issues to a different setting, and so cause frustration and disillusionment to two people instead of just one.

Each person who takes the marriage vows must feel to some degree confident that he or she has something to share, something he or she wants to give to the other person in the marital relationship. As a basic minimum for being wed, there needs to be a discernible joy in a person's life that can be recognized and experienced by others—a sense of joy that is not solely due to the presence of the lover (the person being courted), but stems from many other things in the person's life. Some suggested causes for a person's joy might include: the appreciation of family, the joy of music or art, the inspiration found in reading great books, the beauty of nature, the friendships that have been nurtured through the years, the care of people in need, and especially one's walk with God—to name just a few areas of possibility for joy. Without such a sense of joy in the person wanting to be wed, he/she enters marriage with virtually nothing to share or give, and places on the other person the constant and impossible burden of finding some way of helping the other to experience joy and happiness.

The Christian marriage is a place where we both give and receive. We offer love and are loved. We encourage and are encouraged. So it works best when both partners are able to give delight and joy to the other. When a marriage includes one person (or worse, two) who has (have) a very limited capacity or inclination to be a source of joy to the other, the marriage will be at considerable risk. Or if either the husband or wife has scarcely begun to tap into the excitement of his or her Christian faith and what it means to be obedient to Christ, that marriage will be extremely fragile, like a tiny plant that probably will not be able to survive the heavy downpour of the first storm. Where there is very little knowledge or experience in the life we share in Christ, a couple is merely skirting the heart of a Christian marriage as God intended it to be. His plan is for the man and woman to become one—not only physically, but also spiritually—with both husband and wife having at least a foundational grasp of those qualities referred to in Galatians 5:22–23 as the fruit of the Spirit: love, joy, peace, patience, kindness, goodness, faithfulness, gentleness, and self-control.

Integrating

Our family attended a wedding I conducted. It was our daughter's first time to experience an entire wedding celebration and dinner reception. Later, when we arrived home, we sat in our kitchen relaxing and enjoying a cold drink while sharing our different experiences at the wedding. Sandy was about five years old, and when there was a break in our conversation, she turned to me with excitement in her eyes. "Daddy, do you know what's the fun part of getting married?" I had some ideas but shook my head uncertainly, awaiting her answer. With her head cupped thoughtfully in both hands, she gave me this: "I think the fun part of getting married is when they throw the rice!"

What kinds of experiences cause you joy? Is it whom you are with or what you are seeing or doing that gives you a sense of inward joy? Are you on a merry-go-round with your toddler or enjoying her first train ride? Are you skiing with your spouse and helping your two pre-teens learn how to enjoy this adventuresome sport? Are you playing a board game or card game with treasured close friends?

You Can Find Joy in a Thousand Places

As I have suggested above, each of us finds joy or happiness in many different ways. The possibilities are literally endless—infinite! Like painting a scene from your flower garden in watercolor; canoeing or kayaking through a challenging stretch of rapids;

doing a *New York Times* crossword puzzle on your commute home; taking your three-year-old to feed the ducks at a nearby pond; biking or cycling with your grandson on a favorite trail; doing yard sales or garage sales as a family; making homemade ice cream for a birthday celebration using the family's old hand-cranked ice cream maker; buying a beautiful jigsaw puzzle and assembling it during the course of a quiet weekend; sitting down to enjoy your favorite magazine after getting the kitchen all cleaned up; calling an old friend that you have not talked to for years and laughing together about different experiences; relaxing in the Jacuzzi at the fitness center after a solid workout; biking the countryside over the weekend with several friends; receiving "free tickets" to watch your granddaughters perform in their own dance show in your family room after they've created their own spontaneous choreography to the music provided; deliberately laying down your trowel and garden gloves while gardening, leaning back against a tree to enjoy a breathtaking sunset; arriving home to hear on your answering machine a sweet call from one of your grandchildren thanking you for the extra overnight you sponsored for their family getaway; teaching your nine-year-old how to fly a kite; visiting the library as a family—each person browsing for three books they would like to read and helping one another with the selection; waxing your wife's car and detailing it as a surprise when she returns from a weekend seminar with her girlfriends; shooting baskets with your son and his closest friend; gathering up all of the candles in the house and lighting all of them in your bedroom to surprise your wife when she finishes her shower . . . to cite just a few!

When Sandy was about six years old, we were working outside pruning bushes and raking up leaves. While she was raking, she stopped to reflect, "You know, Daddy, it really is fun to rake, isn't it? But some boys and girls—and some big people too—cannot rake because (here she paused as though she were discovering something for the first time—and wanting to say it right) . . . they cannot—you know—stand up. Or they are too old. Or maybe they do not have one leg. That's sad, isn't it?" I thought about how helpful it is to see life through a child's eyes. What a wondrous gift is health, and what fun it is to rake up leaves in the early fall with sunlight spilling over everything and the wind gently blowing.

If you were to take the time to read the nearly two hundred biblical references to joy, you would discover three resounding themes that serve as helpful hints, cues, or clues as to how we can achieve greater joy in our lives.

1. **The first emphasis of the biblical passages on joy center on the mind-boggling content of the "good news" concerning Jesus.**

What on earth was going on in the heads and hearts of men like John, Thomas, Mark, Paul, and Silas that they took leave of their families and the comfort and security of their homes to walk the world over and tell complete strangers about this Jesus? Those strangers frequently tried to put them in prison—or worse, tried to stone them to death! To answer that question, you need only to get hold of one thing: Jesus one day rose from the dead. These earliest apostles and disciples had met Jesus *after* he had endured the hellish death of cruci-fixion. Or rather, Jesus met them! He met them in an upstairs room rented for special occasions. He met them at the bewilderingly empty tomb. He met them with their tunnel vision on the Emmaus road. He even hosted them at a spontaneous, come-as-you-are breakfast where they could collect themselves after all they had witnessed in Jerusalem when he was crucified. On another occasion, he appeared before some five hundred dropped jaws! The day Jesus was raised from the dead by God's power, the world's inhabitants began to split into two vast camps, those who could believe it happened and those who could not. And these men and women, who understandably were simply called "believers," saw Jesus' resurrection as an indisputable fact—a notable event of history that could be verified by several hundred witnesses.

Moreover, it was an act and a fact that had everything to do with them. In what way? Jesus had explained to them before his death that his rising on the third day was not simply to show God's power, but also to assure them that their own destiny was an eternal one. The uncomplicated truth he gave them could not have been expressed more clearly or more candidly. "In my Father's house are many rooms; if it were not so, I would have told you. I am going there to prepare a place for you. And if I go and prepare a place for you, I will come back and take you to be with me that you also may be where I am" (John 14:2–3).

All that is to say that Jesus' first followers did not have a written theology as the basis for their passionate preaching throughout the inhabited world. Rather, the first Christians had faced a Man whom death could not hold down. These first believers had walked and talked with a Man whom they had carried limp and lifeless to his tomb, yet he reappeared before them alive. These men and women had been served a never-to-be-forgotten breakfast on a familiar beach by One who mastered and overcame death and—except for the scars on his hands and feet—showed no trace of the terror he had endured just three days earlier. In fact, wherever he reappeared as the Resurrected Christ he was recognizable, coherent, and as vital as ever. The basis of their joyous belief was not a literature, but a Life risen from a grave!

2. **When the Scriptures talk about joy, again and again it has to do with our relationships.**

How many experiences of joy stem from our relationships with one another—whether it is our closest friends at church, our marital relationship, our relationships with our children and grandchildren, or with our brothers and sisters or nieces and nephews? Paul, in writing to the church at Philippi, refers to them as his "dear friends" and calls them "my brothers, you whom I love and long for, *my joy and crown*" (Phil. 4:1, emphasis mine). When Paul writes to the church in Corinth, he asks them to "make room for us in your hearts" and then goes on to say, "I have said before that you have such a place in our hearts that we would live or die with you . . . in all our troubles my joy knows no bounds" (2 Cor. 7:2–4). When Paul was passing through one of his worst times, he and his colleagues "had no rest, but . . . were harassed at every turn—conflicts on the outside, fears within" (2 Cor. 7:5b). What is it that breaks their melancholy and puts them on their feet once more? It is the arrival of a very dear friend—Titus. Here is the way Paul experienced renewing his deep friendship with Titus at that discouraging and harrowing hour in his life: "But God, who comforts the downcast, comforted us by the coming of Titus, and not only by his coming but also by the comfort you had given him" (2 Cor. 7:6–7). The gift the Corinthian Christians sent to Paul was not an offering or supplies, but a person, a friend! And this meant so much to the great apostle that he wrote back to Corinth that Titus, "told us about your longing for me, your deep sorrow, your ardent concern for me, *so that my joy was greater than ever*" (2 Cor. 7:7, emphasis mine).

Both the Old and New Testaments give strong testimony that our richest joys in life are to be found in our significant relationships with people. We may not find that to be our experience simply because our priorities in life may have more to do with "getting ahead" in terms of what we earn or own. We may find it difficult to understand how a family with seven children seems so happy, even with all their times of sickness and disrupted nights of sleep. However, if we talked with the father or mother of that family, we very often will hear them attest to the fact that their lives could not have been richer if they had spent them some other way.

3. **The Scriptures also consistently see joy as originating in our personal relationship with God in Jesus Christ.**

For example, when Paul writes from prison to the Christians at Philippi, he does not tell them to rejoice in their *blessings*. Rather, he says, "Rejoice in *the Lord*" (Phil. 3:1; 4:4, emphasis mine). That connection between our God and our joy is made repeatedly in the Scriptures. The prophet Isaiah testifies before Israel, "I delight greatly in the LORD; my soul rejoices in my God" (Isa. 61:10). The psalms frequently begin with this urgent invitation. "Shout for joy to the LORD, all the earth. Worship the LORD with gladness; come before him with joyful songs" (Ps. 100:1–2). Music and singing are often mentioned as the natural accompaniments of our feeling of joy in the Lord. So Psalm 66 begins, "Shout with joy to God, all the earth! Sing the glory of his name; make his praise glorious!" (Ps. 66:1–2). A choir, an orchestra, a brass ensemble, or almost any appropriate combination of instruments may be called into service, as they too help us to express our joy before God and in God. "Sing for joy to God our strength; shout aloud to the God of Jacob! Begin the music, strike the tambourine, play the melodious harp and lyre" (Ps. 81:1; see also Ps. 95:1–2 and 98:6 for similar enthusiastic and jubilant commands).

The Scriptures continually teach us that Jesus is the reason we can rejoice. You cannot think of Jesus apart from the joy he has given us through his graciousness and love. He has made all the difference in the world for us because he has given us his unconditional forgiveness. He has patiently revealed the Father to us through the humility of his incarnation and the clarity of his teachings. He has willingly suffered on our behalf the most excruciating pain through his dying on the cross. Most astonishing of all, he has surprised us through his resurrection from the dead, thereby giving us a glorious future in which we can have hope, for he has told us, "Because I live, you also will live" (John 14:19).

This God-given gift of joy is as indestructible as his love. Hardship and suffering will not rob us of this joy. The prophet Habakkuk speaks forcefully about how our joy remains intact despite the worst of sufferings. His personal statement of faith, which concludes his writings, is inspiring. "Though the fig tree does not bud and there are no grapes on the vines, though the olive crop fails and the fields produce no food, though there are no sheep in the pen and no cattle in the stalls, *yet I will rejoice in the LORD, I will be joyful in God my Savior*" (Hab. 3:17–18, emphasis mine).

A Prayer

Dear God, thanks for all you have done and continue to do to give me fullness of joy. You daily surround me with your beautiful and bountiful gifts—gifts intended to flood my heart with joy. Simple things like the springtime flowers, your couriers of color; glorious things like the pageantry of a sunset composed of fiery reds and tangerine tints streaming their brilliance across darkening skies; or a little child petting a puppy for the very first time! Grant me a greater awareness to notice such things and enjoy them as your personal gifts. I also thank you for the even greater blessings that have so much to do with the way you cherish us—like your gracious capacity to constantly forgive and encourage, and the breathtaking hope of heavenly mansions you are preparing for our everlasting life together. Thanks for all of the joys you have provided this day, through Jesus my Lord. Amen.

Three Questions

1. What most destroys or diminishes our sense of joy in this culture, making joyous experiences fewer and farther apart?

2. If Christ were to suggest to you just one thing that you could begin doing this very week to increase your sense of joy, what specifically do you think would be his starting place for you?

3. What do you think C. S. Lewis meant when he said, "Joy is the serious business of heaven"?

INSIGHTS

Joy is a necessity, not a luxury.

—Harold F. Leestma

Claudel, the French poet, said after listening to Beethoven's Fifth Symphony that he knew now that at the heart of the universe there is joy.

—Gerald Kennedy

People need joy quite as much as clothing. Some of them need it far more.

—Margaret Collier Graham

Joy is the feeling of grinning on the inside.

—Melba Colgrove

The surest mark of a Christian is not faith, or even love, but joy.

—Samuel M. Shoemaker

When I think of God, my heart is so full of joy that the notes leap and dance as they leave my pen; and since God has given me a cheerful heart, I serve him with a cheerful spirit.

—Franz Joseph Haydn

The pursuit of happiness . . . is the greatest feat man has to accomplish.

—Robert Henri

If you could learn how to balance rest against effort, calmness against strain, quiet against turmoil, we would assure ourselves of joy in living and psychological health for life.

—Josephine Rathbone

I love myself when I am laughing.

—Zora Neale Hurston

The general rule is that people who enjoy life also enjoy marriage.

—Phyllis Battelle

CHAPTER THREE

Joseph, a Levite from Cyprus, whom the apostles called Barnabas (which means Son of Encouragement), sold a field he owned and brought the money and put it at the apostles' feet.

—Acts 4:36

ENCOURAGE ONE
ANOTHER

INTERPERSONAL

From the beginning of our dating years, Joanne and I enjoyed writing out our personal feelings for one another, using such occasions as a birthday, Valentine's Day, or Christmas as a time to not only encourage and affirm one another, but also to express our love and appreciation for the one we married. Such personal notes varied in length. The message might have been short, like this one penned on Valentine's Day, or rather lengthy. The potency of such messages is simple. They come from your heart!

> To my wife, Joanne. You are my helpmate in the work of ministry, my encouragement in our most challenging experiences, my partner in prayer and faith, my joy and song in moments of romantic love, and my comfortable companion at all times. With my love, Hubby.

Both Joanne and I try to find special occasion cards that contain a thoughtfully written sentiment with beautiful artwork or photography, but we know that our personal words will have even more meaning than Hallmark's best. Here is a treasured note from my wife on an extraordinarily beautiful card.

Dear Bob, We have shared forty-one married Christmases now, and you have made each one special! I loved our quiet "Christmas for two" years, then the enjoyable Santa Claus Christmases with Sandy, followed by the years of staying up way past midnight (on Christmas Eve) to share Christmas goodies and exchange gifts by the tree. Now we are back to the two of us—a quiet and still romantic time! We have been so blessed. Thanks for being everything a woman could want and long for! I love you! Jo.

Joanne and I never thought to teach this tradition to our daughter, Sandy. Nevertheless Sandy picked up on the idea and practiced it in her own unique style. Below is a sentiment written by her at age ten on a Mother's Day card:

Mom—Jes' wanna thank you for being YOU! "Mother-daughter" times are one of the best parts of life and *you're* what makes them special. HAPPY MOMMY'S DAY! Love ya, Sandy (your favorite daughter!) xoxoxo

(Sandy is our *only* daughter.)

Sandy chose to teach her girls how to express themselves on special occasion cards. To begin this process, she would sit with the girls as a recording secretary, asking them what they would like to say to Grandma, and then writing it down for them. They had the verbal skills to say what they wanted to say, but did not yet have the writing skills to do it without Mom's help. After the "message" was drafted, she would read it back to them, asking, "Is this what you wanted to say?" Her own personal notes as an adult are almost always very specific, concrete, and often consist of vivid memories. Below is a sample penned on a Father's Day card:

Dad—As I was thinking about what to say, I remembered some fun little moments and things I appreciate about you. Buying me a special dress just for me when I was a little girl. Coming to clean my apartment when I was stressed out before the wedding.

Building sandcastles with me. Taking me for cornbread and snacks on our breaks from the library on Saturdays. Lots of special notes. Thank you for being such a faithful Dad and investing so much time and care in me. I Love You! Sandy

These thoughtfully composed personal notes are treasured by our family. And because they are in writing, the recipient can read them years later and again feel encouraged by them!

INSPIRING

After many days had gone by, the Jews conspired to kill him [Saul], but Saul learned of their plan. Day and night they kept close watch on the city gates in order to kill him. But his followers took him by night and lowered him in a basket through an opening in the wall. When he came to Jerusalem, he tried to join the disciples, but they were all afraid of him, not believing that he really was a disciple. But Barnabas took him and brought him to the apostles. He told them how Saul on his journey had seen the Lord and that the Lord had spoken to him, and how in Damascus he had preached fearlessly in the name of Jesus.
—Acts 9:23–27

Men from Cyprus and Cyrene, went to Antioch and began to speak to Greeks also, telling them the good news about the Lord Jesus. The Lord's hand was with them, and a great number of people believed and turned to the Lord. News of this reached the ears of the church at Jerusalem, and they sent Barnabas to Antioch. When he arrived and saw the evidence of the grace of God, he was glad and encouraged them all to remain true to the Lord with all their hearts. He was a good man, full of the Holy Spirit and faith, and a great number of people were brought to the Lord.

Then Barnabas went to Tarsus to look for Saul, and when he found him, he brought him to Antioch. So for a whole year Barnabas and Saul met with the church and taught great numbers of people. The disciples were called Christians first at Antioch.
—Acts 11:20–26

IMAGINING

Public Forum Interview with Barnabas

Antioch, Syria, 34 A.D.

Reporter: We have a few hundred people here today to meet one of the remarkable leaders of the new Christian faith that is currently spreading like wildfire across our Mediterranean world. His name is Joseph of Cyprus, better known as Barnabas, a name which interestingly means "Son of Encouragement." Barnabas, thanks for this opportunity to interview you. First, how did you come upon the name Barnabas?

Barnabas: Well, I think it began as a tease. Those whom I work beside got the idea years ago that my nature was to support the ministry of others. I have never seen leadership as my role, but it makes sense to me that all of us at some time need a word of encouragement. One of my colleagues told me that he saw that as a purpose in my life that I kept coming back to, and so dubbed me "the encourager"—and it somehow stuck.

Reporter: That does seem to fit in terms of yesterday's clash with your leader, the well-known apostle Paul. I understand that after a few years of preaching alongside Paul, the two of you decided to part. Would you share with us the nature of the conflict?

Barnabas: Sure. The conflict has centered on one of our youngest and most promising preachers, a man named Mark. First you have to understand that the work of preaching the good news about Jesus Christ is a controversial and dangerous commitment. I am not talking so much about the usual dangers on the road—such as dealing with an attack by thieves or wild animals, or even a shipwreck at sea. I am referring primarily to the hostility our message occasionally generates. It is not widely known, but the apostle Paul has nearly been killed several times as a result of hostile crowds—the most recent episode being one of our worst experiences to date. A few weeks ago, Paul was nearly stoned to death. A few of us thought he was dead. Younger men like Mark should not be faulted for not staying with this highly dangerous mission.

After being with us for a few months—and I am referring to Mark's first mission circuit with us—he realized how dangerous this work was, and understandably decided to resign and return to his family. I think he discovered how much he was placing his family at risk, and decided that he was not being responsible. I was always able to respect Mark's decision. I never felt that he deserted us.

Reporter: So you're implying that Mark's decision to return home was viewed as an act of cowardice by Paul. Would you share with us the apostle Paul's take on this?

Barnabas: Let me first say that Paul is a courageous and seasoned leader. He's highly motivated by his own relationship with Jesus and tells us that Jesus supplies him with the strength and courage he needs to stay with this costly and risky commitment. More than once we have seen Paul passionately preaching on the streets of a city, with his wounds still conspicuously bandaged. He told me the other day that he feels better when he has bandages on him, because it may make any enemies out there a bit more compassionate toward him! All that is to say Paul has high expectations, not only for himself, but for every team member. In addition, Paul feels strongly that Mark's decision to go back to his home was costly in terms of the overall morale of the team. To make certain that a desertion doesn't reoccur, Paul refuses to accept Mark as a team member. Paul sees him as a liability.

Reporter: So you and Paul have decided that this personal disagreement cannot be compromised. How have you decided to resolve these important differences?

Barnabas: We have been able to work things out satisfactorily. My primary concern was that Mark be given the opportunity to preach the cause of Christ again. I think Mark has had some precious time to think about what he wants to do with his life, and he has discussed and prayed his way through the whole thing, both with his family and with Jesus. Mark now feels convicted that the personal cost, sacrifice, and danger are all worth it. My own perspective is that we are looking at a more mature Mark this time round. He is not the same young man who served with us earlier. I also think history is going to attest to his effectiveness as a preacher.

Reporter: So what does all this mean for your mission as a campaign that's sweeping the whole inhabited world?

Barnabas: In short, Mark and I will go at it together, and have been assigned Cyprus as our target audience. In addition, we agreed that Paul would team up with Silas, another seasoned preacher. They are assigned to Syria and Cilicia. We will continue to keep in touch with them and learn from one another. There are no precedents to guide this mission. As far as I can see, there has never been anything like it in the history of the world. That's why we pause, sometimes several times a day, to pray that we will be subject to Jesus, through the Holy Spirit, and guided by him. This movement does not belong to Paul or to me or to anyone else. It is God's drama, God's dream for his world. We are just doing everything we can to see that his Word is proclaimed to all persons at this critical time.

Reporter: I'm sure that those who are seated in the forum today have picked up the feeling that I have, that you do not really see Jesus as dead. You talk about him as though he were yet alive. Can you help us to understand that better?

Barnabas: Quite honestly, we are still trying to get our minds around that concept ourselves. Every one of the twelve original apostles believed that Jesus died by Roman crucifixion. All of them were brought to despair. When he was crucified, they all felt hopeless and totally disillusioned. They experienced every emotion you can think of from doubt to bitterness, from fear to dread. Then something happened that changed all that. Our team refers to it as "the resurrection." Three days after being buried, Jesus walked out of his hillside tomb. He was seen by all of the apostles in his resurrected or "risen" state. He appeared to more than five hundred believers at one time. I happen to be one of them. It totally changed my life. Our entire mission is driven and energized by that extraordinary experience of Jesus. He is alive again and guiding us.

Reporter: One last question. You have now had many opportunities to preach, and have no doubt learned much from the apostle Paul. How well do you think this new arrangement will work, now that Mark, a young and rather unknown name in this cause, will be working alongside you, a very seasoned and capable preacher?

Barnabas: You have to keep in mind that Jesus was crucified and resurrected less than two years ago. None of us sees himself as a "seasoned" leader or preacher. The whole idea of preaching still feels very new to us. We are all humbled by our calling to this movement. None of us feel especially qualified or know what we should be doing next. We take it a day at a time. I am not sure today where I will be tomorrow. God is doing something so remarkable, so compelling, and exciting that it has literally captured our hearts. We are all bursting with the need to proclaim it to the world. I believe Silas described it once as feeling as if his heart was on fire. We are sure God is fully behind the message we are putting out. After all, it is his idea, and certainly not ours. No mortal could have dreamed up or imagined a God of love who would come down from heaven to be among us, to die for us, and to give us hope of eternal life. Yet, that's what we need to get across. So it is not our preaching that you want to center on and evaluate. You need to focus on the extraordinary things that Jesus is graciously and lovingly doing for all of us.

Reporter: Barnabas, Son of Encouragement, I understand much better why you have been so named. Thanks for being with us today for our forum. I hope you can stay a while to speak with those who might like to hear you address their own questions.

INTERPRETING

Barnabas is mentioned several times in the book of Acts. In nearly every instance, he is an encourager in terms of his actions. His name is first mentioned in Acts 4:36 as the man who sold a field he owned and then brought the money to the apostles, undoubtedly to give tangible support and encouragement to the mission of the fledgling Christian cause. His actual name was Joseph of Cyprus, but he was known throughout the early Christian missionary movement as Barnabas, which means literally "Son of Encouragement." What a wonderful nickname to carry! Did this beautiful name have any influence on the life of Barnabas, actually causing Barnabas to focus on encouragement as a value in his life?

My own family name, *Unverzagt*, comes out of the early German language and means "Never give up!" The meaning was explained to me by a dear saint in her nineties—a dying woman who was fluent in the German language. For years she was too weak to get out of bed and required help with all her needs. As a student minister, I was asked to visit this gentle but physically frail lady of faith. She shared an anecdote with me to help me appreciate my surname. She explained that a farmer would be a long distance from the barn when something failed on his plow or the horses' harnesses. Out there in the hot sun, the farmer would try to fix the problem so that he did not lose precious time coming back to the barn. But after nearly an hour of trying to fix it in some makeshift way, he would finally throw up his arms with exasperation and say, "Verzagt!" which essentially translates, *"I give up!"*

Miss Schickner then turned to me and said more directly, "But your name is just the opposite. It is *Un*-verzagt, which means *'Never give up!'*" She then explained that later in the development of the German language, it came to mean *courageous* or *undaunted*. What a wonderful name to bear! During my thirty-five years of serving troubled churches that had been traumatized by some unfortunate set of circumstances, knowing the meaning of my name was often a helpful reminder to me of my role as a pastor to be courageous, to hold on, to refuse to give up. We are not at all sure how Barnabas's name came about, but it must have had a conscious influence on the person he was becoming year after year. And so it may not be coincidental that Barnabas is so frequently described doing those things that were an encouragement to others.

The second time Barnabas offers encouragement, the scene in Acts is different. Saul, the infamous persecutor of the early church, had been dramatically transformed after the risen Jesus confronted him on the Damascus Road. His conversion and commitment to the way of Jesus immediately became a life-transforming experience. Now his passion was redirected, no less forcefully than his previous commitment to raise "havoc in Jerusalem among those who call on this name [Jesus]" (Acts 9:21). So forceful was Saul as a speaker that a handful of Jews from Damascus conspired to kill him. Saul dramatically escaped the walled city of Damascus by being lowered in a basket from an opening in the wall during the night. It was an effort that succeeded with the help of his newfound Christian friends (see Acts 9:23–25).

We cannot be certain, but it appears likely that Barnabas, and probably others, accompanied Saul to Jerusalem. Saul wished to become a part of the community of believers there and to learn the new Christian faith. The Jerusalem believers had knowledge of Saul's reputation for ruthlessness and could not bring themselves to trust him or to accept him. "They were all afraid of him, not believing that he really was a disciple" (Acts 9:26). At this crucial moment, Barnabas courageously took Saul to the highly skeptical Christian community and introduced him to the believers there, persuading them that Saul was not only a believer, but also a passionate preacher who had been instrumental, through the powerful leading of God's Spirit, in bringing many persons into the new faith. The doubts and tensions dissolved. The believers welcomed this remarkable new convert into the body of Christ. He was a fearless preacher whose personal testimony "grew more and more powerful and baffled the Jews living in Damascus by proving that Jesus is the Christ" (Acts 9:22).

In fact, the Grecian Jews in Jerusalem underestimated Saul's skills as a speaker, and consequently did poorly in an arranged public debate with him. Their next strategy was to deal with this man, whom they regarded as a threat to Judaism rather than its fulfillment, by taking his life. Now we see Barnabas in a very different situation. He is again an encourager, but in a more complex and dangerous situation. It is relatively easy and safe to sell a piece of real estate and then write a check to the church. It is something else to defend the reputation of a man who was a ruthless persecutor. Saul had effectively decimated some of the young Christian communities, resulting in a paralyzing fear.

Barnabas was a strong person who had the courage and integrity to step forward and defend a man with an imposing reputation for creating and heightening fear through his indiscriminate arrests (even to the point of stoning persons to death without a trial). In short, Barnabas not only cleared the way for Saul's personal involvement within the Christian community, with its opportunities for preaching the good news, but he also served as a mediator who brought peace and encouragement to the church itself. He helped it move out of its fearfulness and paralysis to a new confidence in Christ and a resolve to press forward.

Next, we learn that Barnabas became involved in a controversial practice in the early church: preaching the good news of Jesus Christ to Gentiles (people who were not Jews). Great numbers of Gentiles received the gospel and believed. "News of this reached the ears of the church at Jerusalem, and they sent Barnabas to Antioch" (Acts 11:22). This shows how much church leaders respected Barnabas. He was sent to Antioch to witness what the church was doing and bring a report back to Jerusalem. Barnabas probably did not go alone, but he was clearly the person appointed to make an assessment.

What does Barnabas learn when he arrives in Antioch? He surely met a number of the new Gentile converts to Christ. He heard their testimonies and their excitement concerning the good news of Jesus Christ. In those transformed pagan lives, Barnabas "saw the evidence of the grace of God" (Acts 11:23). Barnabas concluded that there was not much difference between a Jewish and a Gentile convert once they became a new man or a new woman in Jesus Christ. Then we read that Barnabas "was glad and encouraged them all [meaning both Jewish and Gentile converts] to remain true to the Lord with all their hearts" (Acts 11:23).

Barnabas must have been invited early on to share in the preaching while he was there, for we next read that Barnabas "was a good man, full of the Holy Spirit and faith, and a great number of people were brought to the Lord" (Acts 11:24). Yet Barnabas had no illusions about his own preaching skills. He soon tentatively excused himself from the preaching mission so he could trek off to Tarsus (a round trip of nearly forty miles) to secure the apostle Paul (formerly known as Saul), whom

Barnabas regarded as the most forceful and passionate preacher of that time. Barnabas personally convinced Paul that he should spend some concentrated time in Antioch, a city that seemed so perfectly ripe for harvest. They then spent an entire year preaching in Antioch, the two men teaching "great numbers of people" (Acts 11:26).

It seems likely that Barnabas modestly saw his role as preacher as secondary to Paul's. In this involvement, Barnabas contributes his own strong personal support and encouragement to the new outreach effort to the Gentiles and willingly participates in the task of preaching. Only after taking his turn in the task of preaching does he step aside to use his personal influence to bring to that city the well-known apostle Paul. Paul comes to Antioch not for just a couple of weeks, but for an entire year as leader of an intense and focused preaching and teaching ministry.

How many persons would have made the decisions Barnabas made? I suspect that others might have been content to stay put and continue preaching, regarding their own gift of preaching too highly to stop and recruit another who had a proven record of drawing countless people into a relationship with Jesus. The reason that Barnabas could be such a remarkable encourager may have been his humble and honest self-appraisal. He knew that he was not an exceptionally strong preacher with Paul's rare capacity. As the New Testament states it, "Do nothing out of selfish ambition or vain conceit, but in humility consider others better than yourselves" (Phil. 2:3). Barnabas did! Barnabas was a team player with the wisdom to know when to step aside and enlist a more capable person. So who should receive the most credit for the incredible growth of the church in Antioch? The apostle Paul? Or was it Barnabas?

The fourth situation in which we see Barnabas as an encourager has to do with his support of Mark, his nephew. Hopefully, most of us would stand beside a nephew who was being treated as a deserter. Knowing Barnabas as we do through the three situations covered above, I suspect he would have still supported Mark even if he had not been his nephew. Would not Barnabas have been compassionate enough to understand why a younger man may have resigned this dangerous work of preaching Christ in a culture that was often hostile, jealous, or threatened by the widespread appeal of the good news concerning Jesus. This young man, whether or not he was a relative, simply needed the opportunity to gain some field experience in preaching and to learn from the more experienced Barnabas how to handle unruly audiences. The gospel of Mark (which is regarded by most biblical scholars as the first gospel to be written) is itself compelling evidence that Barnabas had more insight into the potential of young Mark than any other person on the missionary team, including the great apostle Paul!

INTEGRATING

When it comes to encouraging those around you, is your personality similar to that of Barnabas? Are you an encouragement to your spouse? Persons who are a strong support and encouragement to others—persons like Barnabas—seem to be few in number. Many of us are so preoccupied with our own struggles in life that we have little energy or imagination left to offer a few well-chosen words of affirmation or encouragement to another.

Years ago my wife was diagnosed with a lump in her breast that required surgery. Following surgery she was informed through a follow-up mammogram that the tumor was at least partially still there. The surgeon had successfully removed only a part of it. We decided to seek out another surgeon to deal with the problem. The new surgeon we chose not only had high qualifications, she was also a tremendous support to Joanne in terms of her personal skills. She was able to listen, comfort, and encourage. After the corrective surgery was successfully completed, Joanne wrote the surgeon a lengthy thank you note telling her how much she appreciated her time, sensitivity, and encouragement to get her through one of the most traumatic experiences of her life. She also thanked her for her competence, dedication, and years of gathering experience in her practice.

Weeks later, Joanne had her follow-up appointment, during which the surgeon thanked my wife for her thoughtful note. The surgeon then added, "I have been practicing for twenty-two years and your personal note of thanks was the first I have ever received. I really appreciate your thoughtfulness in taking the time to write such a lovely note." If this surgeon's experience is typical, we are missing a tremendous opportunity to build up people.

In strong contrast we have Jesus, undoubtedly the greatest encourager who ever lived! Ten lepers, who apparently knew something about Jesus' healings, once came to him pleading for the healing of their leprosy. Jesus healed all ten of them (see Luke 17:11–19). Just minutes after their request, they were healed. No longer were they feared for their loathsome look. Their ugly sores had vanished and their skin was like that of a newborn baby. Ten miracles experienced by ten lepers. Yet only one thanked Jesus for the awesome healing of this terrible disease that had isolated them from the larger community.

Jesus had the power to heal persons, and he gave that gift freely and fully to those who were sick, paralyzed, blind, epileptic, or leprous. It did not matter whether the sick or diseased person was a Jew or a Gentile, a man or a woman, an adult or a child, wealthy or poor. I suspect that the ten lepers were ten very different personalities— a company made up of the courageous and the complaining; the humble and the hostile; the questioner and the quiet one; the man filled with despair, as well as the man who believed each day that he would someday be healed. It did not matter to Jesus. *He healed every one of them.* He healed every one of them *completely.* He held back nothing.

Not only did Jesus bring great encouragement to such persons in particular; he also gave every man, woman, and child on this planet, and persons of generations yet unborn, the greatest encouragement imaginable through his death on the cross that cost him everything, to pay for our sins; and his words of hope about life eternal that we could find in him, if we simply trust his words. Jesus is the greatest encourager we have ever seen. Perhaps Jesus wants to encourage you in your marriage and have you learn from him how to be an encourager with your spouse.

How Can You Encourage Your Spouse?

The particular ways in which we encourage another human being differ because our personalities are different. At the beginning of this chapter, I shared some of our family's personal notes to one another on occasions such as Christmas, Father's Day, or a birthday. These notes may take different forms. I once gave my wife a birthday card that had large margins around the printed message, but no open space to write out some of my special feelings about her. The format of this card forced me to come up with another way of communicating my personal message. I came up with the idea of "ballooned" thoughts that could be written in the ample margins, each highlighted with a penned "cloud" around them. I noted things I personally enjoyed doing with her:

- Sharing together Charis and Syd's first time at reading a children's book *to us*.
- Landscaping our garden areas on a bright, sunny day.
- Receiving a surprise, no-occasion gift from you when you arrived home from shopping.
- Caring for one another through broken arms, backaches, the flu, vertigo, emergency rooms, and surgeries.
- Bringing an ice-cold soda and snack to you while sunning at poolside.
- Christmas shopping at our favorite mall and stopping for hot chocolate to review our list.
- A warm morning kiss to start the day!

We are limited only by our imagination. When I started writing this book my wife thoughtfully encouraged me by giving me a beautiful black attaché case with several compartments for books, legal pads, organizers, and pens so that I could easily take my project to the library, the local park, the seashore, or my favorite coffee shop. Here are a few ideas to help stir your own creative thoughts:

- Write a brief love message on the mirror your husband uses to shave in the morning. You might want to select a lipstick you no longer need or prefer. Add a couple of artful hearts or red lips signifying a kiss. Place it on the mirror so it does not entirely obstruct his ability to see himself. Make the message as short or as long as you wish, but take into consideration who, besides your husband, may read the message should he choose to save it for a week.

- Arrange to "steal" your wife's car so you can vacuum, polish, and detail it as a surprise when she returns from a get together with girlfriends or a weekend seminar or retreat that does not require her to be the driver. When presenting it to her, you may want to park it on an angle on your lawn. Be careful not to give the impression that it's a new car, or she could be disappointed instead of delighted. Write a brief note and tape it to the driver's door or the dash to say something encouraging and affirming. Here is an illustration: "Cath, I appreciate all the time you spent over the past year making medical appointments and tracking all the follow-up therapies and medical bills for Debra. We will get through this! Love, Ken."

- When your husband has helped with a rash of repairs that are occurring with frustrating frequency (getting a new hot water heater hooked up, replacing a defective light switch on the basement stairwell, etc.), encourage him with a love note. "Larry, thanks for your extra attention to all the projects around this old house that have kept you on the run recently. Can we get the kids to bed early tonight because I'd like to make you *my* special project! Love, Liz."

- Pick up several of your wife's favorite snacks or candies at a store that sells bulk candy so you can present most of them without all the advertising and product names, adding a note to the basket or gift bag. Here's an instance: "Marie, you are the sweetest helpmate imaginable! Thanks for all your extra help with the kids while I have been trying to get Mom settled into her cozier, downsized house. Hang in there! We are almost home—no pun intended! Love ya, Wayne."

- A simple winter idea! Pick up a can of de-icer at an auto store and put a note on it as a fun no-occasion gift; "Glenn, I know you hate these terribly cold mornings since the record-breaking snow hit us, so this is to make it a little easier to get off to work with a little less scraping. Incidentally, I love the way you warm me up on a winter night! Love, Amy."

- Bundle together with transparent tape or ribbon a trio of her favorite salty snacks (Bavarian pretzels, old-fashioned kettle-cooked potato chips, a canister of cashew nuts, etc.) with your love note or words of encouragement attached. Here's one. "Danise, I admire all the time you're spending with your Aunt Tillie while she's going through this difficult time. I know she's not always very appreciative, but the Lord and I have both noticed all your loving ways, and also know that our children have to be learning something good from this. I love you! Tom. P.S. 'You are the salt of the earth.'"

While I was volunteering once with Lend A Hand in D'Iberville, Mississippi, doing a week-long service project (with about thirty other volunteers) rebuilding homes severely damaged by super-hurricane Katrina, my wife tucked a few love notes between my folded shirts. One said, "Bob, if it is Thursday or Friday when you find this note, you're most likely not changing your shirts frequently enough! I love you and miss you! Joanne." You might be surprised just how much joy, warmth, and laughter can come to your marriage by a simple note on the pillow or in a lunch bag or tucked strategically in the sock drawer!

Of course, our encouragement need not be in the form of an attaché case or a can of de-icer. It may be simply an experience—taking your wife out to dinner when she is facing a critical review of her position at work. Or it may be an experience in which we use our time and skills to encourage our spouse. A friend of mine, Terry Stephens, once offered his time and considerable technical skills to enable me to mount a beautiful vanity top and decorative faucet in our upstairs bathroom—part of a modest bathroom makeover given to my wife as a boxed Christmas gift, with a promise to install it!

Another friend of mine, Fred Moore, helped me paint the trim on our home during a time when he was unemployed. He gave me some very helpful tips and skills that have ever since reduced the frustration that typically was a part of any painting job. The blue painter's tape and the new paint additives that enable the paint brush to perform much easier are now resources that have raised my painting skills from, "I will get through this," to, "Let me show you what I did to our garage last week!" You do not have to wait until Christmas to be an encouragement to someone!

Whatever you decide to do should be exciting for you, whether it is simple and easy to put together or is more time-consuming and costly. If it feels as if it is going to be a burden, you might want to spend another day or so to do some creative brooding. You need to first come up with an idea that really turns you on, so that you can't wait to get it underway! And do not forget to warmly accept, acknowledge, and show your personal appreciation when your spouse does something that encourages you.

A Prayer

Lord, I thank you for the unique personal skills and gifts that you have given to me to serve you and to freely share with others. I am grateful for those who have been an encouragement to me through the years—especially those who have helped me to mature as a person, to grow in my faith, and to stretch myself more in terms of loving and encouraging others. Especially show me ways in which I can be an encouragement to my wife (husband). Help me to keep my eyes on Jesus, your Son, as the greatest encourager ever to walk this planet. Teach me to give of myself more freely, just as Jesus did when he healed the ten lepers who appealed to him for mercy. In his glorious name I pray. Amen.

Three Questions

1. Think of a time when someone really encouraged you. What were the circumstances, what happened, how were you encouraged? Was it a note, help with a frustrating project, or simply time spent together when you were going through a difficult problem?

2. Imagine this is a time in your marriage when you are dealing with unemployment, and you are without your main source of income. Can you come up with two ideas that would allow you to offer creative encouragement with no outlay of money, or at most only a few dollars?

3. If money posed no restrictions whatever, and you had all the time in the world, what would you like to give your husband, or wife, as an expression of your personal encouragement?

INSIGHTS

Encouragement is oxygen to the soul.

—George M. Adams

[Christ] died for us so that . . . we may live together with him. Therefore encourage one another and build each other up, just as in fact you are doing.

—1 Thess. 5:10–11

If I cannot give my children a perfect mother, I can at least give them more of the one they've got—and make that one more loving. I will be available. I will take time to listen, time to play, time to be home when they arrive from school, time to counsel and encourage.

—Ruth Bell Graham

I have never seen a man who could do real work except under the stimulus of encouragement and enthusiasm and the approval of the people for whom he is working.

—Charles M. Schwab

The sweetest of all sounds is praise.

—Xenophon

Every day, tell at least one person something you like, admire, or appreciate about them.

—Richard Carlson

CHAPTER FOUR

Therefore let us stop passing judgment on one another. Instead, make up your mind not to put any stumbling block or obstacle in your brother's way.

—Rom. 14:13

Changing Yourself—
Not Your Mate

INTERPERSONAL

During the first several years of our marriage, I thought it was appropriate to encourage my wife to be a better person. After all, we were now in a very intimate relationship as marriage partners. Are we not to be constantly maturing as committed Christians?

For example, I wanted her to be more adventurous. The year I wanted to buy a pre-owned 1966 Oldsmobile Toronado with its incredibly sleek lines and retractable headlights, Joanne was opposed to buying it. Because it had so many options that could require service, she was absolutely convinced it would always be in the shop for repairs.

In addition to becoming more adventurous, I also wanted her to feel more secure. She was always locking doors. One day I took the trash out and when I returned the door was locked! I also encouraged her to exercise—walk, jog, or bike on a faithfully kept schedule. Joanne had no interest in exercise and when she gained some fifteen extra pounds during our middle years, I thought our marriage was entering a crisis stage!

It took a long time for me to understand that God had chosen to give me a wife and not a clone of myself. How boring my marriage would have been if my spouse had only my interests and viewed life exactly as I did.

The more experience I have as a marriage partner, the more I appreciate why God has made the man and woman *complementary* and not *identical*. Our first clue on this matter is the obvious differences in our physical appearance and capacities. Observing that, why would we expect our personalities, perspectives, or priorities to be exactly the same?

Besides, the woman I fell in love with never had signed up for an exercise program while I was romancing her. Joanne felt that life was too precious to spend a significant slice of every week to have a flat tummy! As for keeping doors securely locked, we admittedly are living in a bizarre and violent time requiring caution and vigilance. Joanne never had the need to impress anyone with her choice of clothes or car or to spend her money on anything frivolous. Besides, the Toronado, as it turned out, *was* always in the shop for repairs!

We will find much more adventure, excitement, and joy in our marriages as we surrender our secret ploy to change our spouses. Leave that complex task in the hands of God, and instead concentrate on life's most challenging and fulfilling enterprise—pursuing with all our heart, mind, and strength to become more Christlike ourselves.

INSPIRING

If anyone else thinks he has reasons to put confidence in the flesh, I have more: circumcised on the eighth day, of the people of Israel, of the tribe of Benjamin, a Hebrew of Hebrews; in regard to the law, a Pharisee; as for zeal, persecuting the church; as for legalistic righteousness, faultless.

But whatever was to my profit I now consider loss for the sake of Christ. What is more, I consider everything a loss compared to the surpassing greatness of knowing Christ Jesus my Lord, for whose sake I have lost all things. I consider them rubbish, that I may gain Christ and be found in him, not having a righteousness of my own that comes from the law, but that which is through faith in Christ—the righteousness that comes from God and is by faith. I want to know Christ and the power of his resurrection and the fellowship of sharing in his sufferings, becoming like him in his death, and so, somehow, to attain to the resurrection from the dead. Not that I have already obtained all this, or have already been made perfect, but I press on to take hold of that for which Christ Jesus took hold of me. Brothers, I do not consider myself yet to have taken hold of it.

But one thing I do: Forgetting what is behind and straining toward what is ahead, I press on toward the goal to win the prize for which God has called me heavenward in Christ Jesus.

—Phil. 3:4–14

IMAGINING

God Changed Himself for Our Sake?

Can you believe that God could thrust into the blackness of space
The mighty mass of the planet Pluto—
Trained to obey the galaxy's giddy laws of gravity and relativity,
Somersaulting smoothly and silently on an invisible track,
As though weightless as a balloon,
Effortlessly gulping up millions of miles
Laid out in one vast incomprehensible circle—
Unerringly keeping its hypnotizing rotation through a million years
    of darkness?

Can you believe that God could thrust into the protective chamber of
    a woman's womb
The incubated mystery of life,
Particles of matter weightless and unseen,
And by the whisper of his Word,
Transform it into eyes and ears and a beating heart
Particles becoming a person
Whose mind might create a symphony,
Whose hands could defeat death with a scalpel,
Whose spirit would discern the voice of God?

Can you believe that God could thrust into the shadows of a stable
The Light of the world—
A portrait of Himself so vivid and faithful
That the centuries have not blurred the stirring thought
Of the Infinite transfigured into an Infant,
Our Creator mysteriously sent down from the magnificent mansions
      of heaven
To stand no higher than a man's gaze,
To walk in the very center of everything He created
So as to give us his love and his life
On a cross?

INTERPRETING

I have no idea how I came to believe that our marriage would be better if I could convince my wife to do certain things that were important to me. This desire to change others probably springs out of our sinful and fallen nature and finds a beachhead for operations in our selfishness. The Word does not offer a single thought to encourage us to change our spouses. We may share how God is working within us through the Holy Spirit to transform us into one who is becoming hopefully more and more Christlike. But sharing where we are spiritually in our journey with Christ is not at all the same as exhorting, prodding, or nagging a mate to change behavior so as to be a greater blessing to oneself.

The Scriptures address us directly and personally. "You are the light of the world," Jesus affirms. "Let your light shine before men, that they may see your good deeds and praise your Father in heaven" (Matt. 5:14–16). It does not say, "Urge your wife to be the light of the world so you can enjoy her good deeds done for your own personal satisfaction." The Word says, "Be kind and compassionate to one another, forgiving each other, just as in Christ God forgave you" (Eph. 4:32). It does not say, "Keep pushing your mate to be kind, compassionate, and forgiving so you can enjoy a happier life with her." The Scriptures say, "Above all, my brothers, do not swear . . . let your 'Yes' be yes, and your 'No,' no" (James 5:12). It does not say, "Wives, if you have a husband who has a habit of swearing, keep on his case until he stops using such objectionable language." If persons became more loving and more sensitive as a result of their partner's efforts to change them, we would have countless millions of happier and healthier marriages. We are not called to transform others, but to be transformed ourselves by God. Transforming is God's work alone.

The apostle Paul writes to the church in Rome, "Therefore let us stop passing judgment on one another. Instead, make up your mind not to put any stumbling block or obstacle in your brother's way" (Rom. 14:13). The *JB Phillips New Testament* translation paraphrases it and gives the statement more clarity and power. "Let us therefore stop turning critical eyes on one another. If we must be critical, let us be critical of our own conduct and see that we do nothing to make a brother stumble or fall" (Rom. 14:13).[4]

When I was in my forties, I wrote in my journal, "Lord, seal my lips against all that is negative and critical." I had no idea how difficult that would be to live out. Many times have I prayed some variation of that same prayer. It is so easy to criticize another person. But it is totally counterproductive. Anyone who is married will take a giant step forward to a happier marriage on the day they begin to pray, "*Lord, if I must be critical, let me be critical of my own conduct, my own attitudes, my own ways of relating to my wife/ husband.*"

There is another aspect of this verse that is important to understand. Paul's plea in Romans 14:13 *commands* us to give up a widespread behavior that feels almost natural to us. Moreover, many of us have been doing it for so many years that it's entwined and ingrained in our personality and behaviors. Emotionally, many seem to be always ready to "turn a critical eye" on others. Therefore, the habit is extremely difficult to change.

Because we are commanded to "stop passing judgment on one another," such a change in behavior depends upon our will, not our emotional mood. We likely will never be in the mood to turn our critical skills on ourselves. The success of doing so depends upon our holding the conviction that this is God's way for us. It has to be worked out in our heads and not in the flight of our emotions. Eventually our emotional side will love our new life that no longer finds satisfaction in criticizing others. In the beginning, however, we will need to tug it along like a leashed dog not wanting to go back home. So we need to accept this as God's plan for our growth to maturity and our greater joy. "Do not conform any longer to the pattern of the world, but be transformed by the renewing of your mind" (Rom. 12:2). That is to say, *your* mind, and no one else's.

While out walking years ago, I remember resting for a few minutes to read some college postings on a massive dormitory door. A thumbtacked index card bore this thought: "We made Jesus into the perfect Son of God so as to excuse ourselves from any deep sense of obligation to live out our lives at the same lofty heights which he had attained." I, of course, believe that Jesus *is* the perfect Son of God and did not graduate to that position as a result of how people viewed his earthly life. Other than that, the statement is thought provoking.

If you're looking for a lifestyle that is a cakewalk, you will not find it in Jesus. He wants us "to live out our lives at the same lofty heights which he had attained." In him we are to forgive unconditionally, persevere through all our troubles, and do so joyfully and without complaining. We are to give generously of our resources, serve others by using our unique gifts for their benefit, love others as much as we love ourselves, and graciously cut some slack for others rather than criticizing or condemning them. We strive to attain such a lifestyle over much of our lifetime.

In the Philippians 3:5–6 passage in which Paul seems to be boasting about his credentials when he says, "Of the tribe of Benjamin, a Hebrew of the Hebrews; in regard to the law, a Pharisee . . . as for legalistic righteousness, faultless," he is really trying to teach his readers two things. In the first place, all the things having to do with power, prestige, and pedigree, Paul comes to see in a different light when he surrenders his life to Jesus Christ. "I consider them rubbish, that I may gain Christ and be found in him" (Phil. 3:8–9). Our college or university degrees with their prized *cum laude* or *valedictorian* recognition, and our titles of President of the Board of Directors or CEO for the corporation one day pale when our eyes are opened to "the surpassing greatness of knowing Christ Jesus my Lord" (Phil. 3:8).

His second point has to do with his new direction or focus. Paul now wants to become like Christ, knowing fully how unreachable and unattainable are the virtues and principles that Jesus has provided through his example. Nevertheless, he is deliberately on a new course to pursue them. His new course is marked by humility. Although Paul is now the leader of the movement to spread the good news of Jesus Christ throughout the entire inhabited world, he maintains a very modest understanding of himself in the light of knowing Christ as his Lord. "Not that I have already obtained all this, or have already been made perfect, but I press on to take hold of that for which Christ Jesus took hold of me" (Phil. 3:12).

And just in case we have missed what he is now working toward, he restates it a second time. And note how his newly-found goal in life has nothing whatever to do with changing others but rather has everything to do with his own growth and his personal relationship to Jesus Christ. "Brothers, I do not consider myself yet to have taken hold of it. But one thing I do: Forgetting what is behind and straining toward what is ahead, I press on toward the goal to win the prize for which God has called me heavenward in Christ Jesus" (Phil. 3:13–14). What wonderful marriages we would see if only both husbands and wives understood clearly that their own growth in Christ is their primary push, the "one thing" they need to be doing.

Because of our eternal destiny in Jesus Christ, he will continually, faithfully, and unhesitatingly nudge us toward fullness of life. "Be perfect," Jesus urges, "as your heavenly Father is perfect" (Matt. 5:48). Once we accept that challenge, we will have so much to do that we will no longer have time to alter or make over someone else's life!

INTEGRATING

The Bible constantly calls us to change. The concepts of repentance and forgiveness both suggest and assume that we need to make changes in our lives. "You were taught, with regard to your former way of life, to put off your old self, which is being corrupted by its deceitful desires; to be made new in the attitude of your minds; and to put on the new self, created to be like God in true righteousness and holiness" (Eph. 4:22–24). Paul, writing to the infant church in Galatia, says, "Neither circumcision nor uncircumcision means anything; what counts is a new creation" (Gal. 6:15). There are countless Scriptures in both the Old and New Testaments which call for changes in our attitudes and behaviors. "Get rid of all bitterness, rage and anger, brawling and slander, along with every form of malice. Be kind and compassionate to one another, forgiving each other, just as in Christ God forgave you" (Eph. 4:31–32).

Moreover, these changes are not cosmetic or trivial. They ultimately amount to a complete overhaul. "Therefore, if anyone is in Christ, he is a new creation; the old has gone, the new has come!" (2 Cor. 5:17). If we want a happier marriage, our prayer needs to be that of the psalmist: "Create *in me* a pure heart, O God, and renew a steadfast spirit *within me*" (Ps. 51:10, emphasis mine).

But how do we become motivated to do this important work of being transformed by God? As I write this chapter, I am engaged in what I call a health and fitness initiative. I call it that smilingly because it sounds much better than, "I'm finally getting back to exercising, which I have neglected for months." How can we become excited about launching a spiritual life and character initiative, getting back to maturing as a person in Christ?

How do you see your role as a wife or husband, as a mom or dad, as the hostess at a restaurant or the CEO of a corporation? Do you aim toward excellence in any of these roles? I don't know of anyone who is striving to be mediocre. But neither do I know of many who are striving for excellence. It seems that most of us admire the flawless performance of a gold medalist or the paraplegic who has learned considerable painting techniques using only her teeth and lips to guide the brush. We admire the creative mind that has successfully organized thousands of people in dozens of countries to build affordable homes for the poor. We enjoy listening to our favorite singers, reading bestsellers, and watching the icons of our favorite sports perform skillfully and courageously, the slow motion camera showing in detail the amazing catch! However, too seldom do we ourselves aspire to being the best husband in town or the best wife ever.

Have you ever taken on such a quest, such a vision for yourself? "Let us therefore stop turning critical eyes on one another. If we must be critical, let us be critical of our own conduct and see that we do nothing to make a brother stumble or fall" (Rom. 14:13 JB Phillips New Testament).

What aspects of your life will you do with excellence? Will you be guided by God's instructions for your role as husband or wife so that God will be glorified by your life and your children will have clear role models for their own future roles, whatever they may be? What will you be remembered for in the end?

I hope to be remembered as a builder—rebuilding homes damaged by hurricane and flooding, encouraging their distressed and depressed homeowners, and rekindling the fire and passion in hurting marriages. Our world is not doing too well with our current stream of celebrity types, whether they are the popular sports figures or the glamorous titans of our most celebrated movies. You and I may never have a national audience observing our faith and values, but we could surely make a difference in the network of those many persons who make up the seamless and interacting influence of our very visible and influential lives.

What if God called you to be a friend and advocate of the disabled by developing a unique business that exists not to make you a millionaire, but to enable wheelchair dependent persons to support themselves and their families with a livable wage and benefits, doing work that is purposeful and valuable to the community? What if God called you to manage your six-digit salary and lifestyle so you could build several schools in an impoverished country like Ghana, Africa?

Suppose God called you to be the hospitality person in your church, always at the door warmly welcoming first-time visitors and remembering them by name. Suppose God called you to encourage corporations to donate computers for children in inner city school districts with inadequate budgets, enlisting honor students to volunteer their time to teach children how to increase their computer skills and appreciate how this tool can do incredible things, including changing their lifestyle and earning capacity. Suppose God inspired you and your spouse to be a striking example of an exciting marriage that is clearly rooted or re-rooted in Christ and taking the Scriptures seriously in terms of focusing on such qualities as joyfulness, selflessness, graciousness, encouragement, and forgiveness—one at a time. And if you accepted such a nudge by God, would your life move from bland and dull to an exciting and a mutually shared atmosphere of joyousness and personal fulfillment?

Should you prayerfully conclude or decide that God is inviting you (or better, both of you) to transformation through the clear guidance of the Holy Spirit active in our hearts, and you wish to adapt to the new task of changing yourself and not your mate, here are a few suggestions:

- *Share the change of view with your spouse.* Ask him/her to be patient with you because you will be trying to make a major shift in your role as husband/wife, and it is not likely to happen overnight. Our longstanding habits are not easily modified or quickly exchanged.
- *Pray that God will enable you to maintain your new vision.* Keep in mind that the process of transforming is the work of God and is achieved by the Holy Spirit residing within us, guiding us, encouraging us, and perfecting us through his power at work within us, renewing our minds.
- *Do not be tempted to take the shortcut of following a couple you admire.* Every marriage is different, made up of different personalities and histories, different responsibilities, differing experiences, and differing conflicts and needs. Learn to be guided directly by God's indwelling Spirit who knows precisely what your marriage needs and will faithfully lead you step by step. God has chosen to guide us himself so that we can benefit from true wisdom and not something inaccurate or inadequate from even the most mature couple among our friends.

A Prayer

Lord Jesus, you wanted to be close to your disciples, and so you walked with them from town to town as you went about your ministry. As you walked to Emmaus, you gave up solitude to walk with two men who were struggling to understand what was happening in Jerusalem that related to their faith in God. You set up a breakfast gathering on the beach to fellowship with fishermen coming in from a discouraging night of hard work. I think I'm beginning to catch what you want to do with me and my spouse. Close friendships don't just happen. They require some time to be with each other, to share and laugh, and even to cry at times. Friends must also learn from each other and encourage one another. Isn't that what you're offering me and my wife/husband? We cannot really fulfill your plan for our marriage until we are humble enough to seek you with all our hearts. You want to give us your own prescription much as our family physician does when we are feeling sick. Lord, I want to begin to pay greater attention to your exciting plan for our life as a couple, a plan that will give me much to ponder and learn. In order to have the time to do that faithfully, day by day and week by week, I surrender all my time and effort in trying to change my mate. So help me, God, through Jesus Christ my Lord. Amen.

Three Questions

1. Why does God want to guide our marriage relationship much like a private tutor? Why do you suppose he chose to offer every couple a one-on-one relationship with him rather than simply depending on the teaching ministry of the church to instruct our marital role?

2. How should a Christian couple see their role when another couple seeks their advice about a serious problem that is presently causing a struggle in their marriage?

3. Are you guilty or innocent in terms of the tendency to try to upgrade your spouse and encourage him/her to be a better person or a better marriage partner?

Insights

Everybody thinks of changing humanity and nobody thinks of changing himself.

—Leo Tolstoy

You will never be an inwardly religious and devout man unless you pass over in silence the shortcomings of your fellow men, and diligently examine your own weaknesses.

—Thomas A. Kempis

A proud man is always looking down on things and people, and, of course, as long as you're looking down, you can't see something that's above you.

—C. S. Lewis

Search thy own heart; what paineth thee in others in thyself may be.

—John Greenleaf Whittier

A critic is one who would have you write it, sign it, paint it, play it, or carve it as he would—if he could.

—Author Unknown

Most people are searching for happiness. They're looking for it. They're trying to find it in someone or something outside of themselves. That's a fundamental mistake. Happiness is something that you are, and it comes from the way you think.

—Wayne Dyer

Not being beautiful was the true blessing . . . Not being beautiful forced me to develop my inner resources. The pretty girl has a handicap to overcome.

—Golda Meir

Accept one another, then, just as Christ accepted you, in order to bring praise to God.

—Rom. 15:7

CHAPTER FIVE

Then Joseph threw his arms around his brother Benjamin and wept, and Benjamin embraced him, weeping. And he kissed all his brothers and wept over them. Afterward his brothers talked with him.

—Gen. 45:14–15

A Spectacular Forgiveness

INTERPERSONAL

During the first few years of our marriage, I can remember feeling frustration or anger over something my wife said or did. The anger was intense enough to spoil our relationship for a day or two, and occasionally suspending our lovemaking for a night or two. Ironically, while I can easily recall the feeling of being hurt or aggravated and the feeling of tense uneasiness and awkward silence, I cannot recall the particular issue that triggered my argumentative and defensive attitude and the accompanying collision of wills.

Yet I was stubborn enough to surrender much of the warmth and companionship of our relationship and even the wonder and joy of lovemaking for some issue that now I cannot even recall! Was it that my wife forgot to post a payment in our checkbook register that resulted in an overdrawn account? Had she asked me too many times to see what I could do with the leak in the bathroom? I really do not remember. But I feel thankful that at some point I matured a little and am no longer repeating that piece of foolishness!

When we had been married ten years, I was serving as a youth pastor in Milltown, New Jersey. The senior pastor was to be away for a few weeks, and I was trusted with many of his responsibilities, including preaching. Our daughter, Sandy, only a few months old,

71

became very sick on a Sunday I was to preach, so Joanne stayed home to care for her. And she also used the morning to catch up on laundry. She threw some of our clothing items, including a dress shirt of mine that secretly bore my petite pocket calendar, into the washer!

By the time I arrived home, Joanne had discovered and retrieved most of the soaked and wrinkled bits and pieces of my pocket calendar, and already was undertaking the considerable challenge of flattening and organizing the hundreds of shredded pieces of pages across our kitchen table. She was making very little progress despite her best efforts at reconstructing pages of blurred writing. Before I could even get to the kitchen, she was preparing me by throwing out a hope she held. "I hope your sermon was on *forgiveness* today!" Stepping into our kitchen, I answered: "No, my topic was honesty. Why do you ask?" Looking at me she said, "Well, quite *honestly,* I just laundered your datebook!"

It did not require many words to explain what happened and we both had a good laugh! It was a fun story that we often shared with friends through the years. I remember it as a symbolic turning point in my life as a marriage partner. Years earlier I would have fumed over what had happened and would have treated her as if she were less than a responsible person. This time I responded by sitting down and helping her reassemble my datebook that had become a 500-piece, water-soaked and wrinkled paper puzzle without an accompanying picture to guide us!

How would you rate yourself as a marriage partner when it comes to cutting slack, overlooking mistakes, forgiving, making allowances, or letting it slide?

INSPIRING

Then Joseph could no longer control himself before all his attendants, and he cried out, "Have everyone leave my presence!" So there was no one with Joseph when he made himself known to his brothers. He wept so loudly that the Egyptians heard him, and Pharaoh's household heard about it. Joseph said to his brothers, "I am Joseph! Is my father still living?" His brothers were unable to answer him, because they were terrified at his presence. Then Joseph said to his brothers, "Come close to me." When they had done so, he said, "I am your brother Joseph, the one you sold into Egypt! And now, do not be distressed and do not be angry with yourselves for selling me here because it was to save lives that God sent me ahead of you. For two years now there has been famine in the land, and for the next five years there will be no plowing and reaping. But God sent me ahead of you to preserve for you a remnant on earth and to save your lives by a great deliverance. So then, it was not you who sent me here, but God. He made me father to Pharaoh, lord of his entire household and ruler of all Egypt. . . . You can see for yourselves, and so can my brother Benjamin, it is really I who am speaking to you. Tell my father about all the honor accorded me in Egypt and about everything that you have seen. And bring my father down here quickly." Then he threw his arms around his brother Benjamin and wept, and Benjamin embraced him, weeping. And he kissed all his brothers and wept over them. Afterward his brothers talked with him.

—Gen. 45:1–8, 12–15

IMAGINING

Joseph could no longer control his emotions as he stood there unrecognized in the presence of all his brothers, Benjamin included. He wanted so much to embrace Benjamin and openly share everything that was on his heart. (Joseph and Benjamin, you may recall, were the sons of Rachel and so shared a special place in Jacob's heart.) All of his brothers had no idea they were standing before Joseph, their own brother, the one they had so angrily sold to the Ishmaelite slave traders.

Looking back over his life, Joseph was more certain than ever that God had planned for him to save many lives in the extensive famine that oppressed not only Egypt, but surrounding countries as well. However, there had been many nights in Joseph's earlier years when he sat chained on a stone floor of a dungeon, feeling miserable and confused as he desperately tried to make sense out of all that had happened to him. Why had God allowed his own brothers to sell him into slavery when he was only seventeen years of age? Why had he been unjustly accused by Potiphar's wife when he had tried to be faithful to Potiphar by refusing her aggressive sexual advances? And then, within hours, her dramatic lies had effectively sealed his imprisonment.

Joseph had been serving Pharaoh for nine years. The powers given to him were astonishing. At times he had felt overwhelmed, for he had been raised as a shepherd boy, his youth spent tending sheep. During his royal ministry to Pharaoh, Joseph had plenty of time to think. He had come, little by little, to the conclusion that it wasn't Pharaoh who made him prime minister of Egypt—it was God. It was God who patiently waited, making sure that Joseph was mature enough to handle the immense task of guiding a major nation through seven years of severe famine. It was God who exchanged Joseph's naïveté and self-absorbed personality as a youth for the priceless virtues of humility, patience, perseverance, and wisdom. These foundations of character had been acquired by Joseph as he experienced the pain of injustice, combined with long years of solitude behind prison walls. It was God and only God who had enabled him to precisely interpret dreams that had been obscure to others. And now, once again, God had not only sent his brothers down to Egypt for grain, he had also arranged for them to be discovered in the thick of the crowds by the only person in Egypt who could have possibly recognized them—*Joseph!* All this he well understood.

What he did not so clearly understand was how he should go about revealing who he was to his brothers. What should he say to them? In recent months, Joseph had vacillated over these personal issues. Seeing his brothers once again after more than twenty years had awakened within him a torrent of emotions. His anger was rekindled as he recalled the ruthless and merciless way they had discarded him from their lives, cut off with virtually no possibility of ever seeing home again. He was also stirred with a feeling of compassion for their alarming situation back in Canaan. How was the family managing during this bleak and unrelenting famine, especially since they had no idea that it would continue five more years? He also felt a strong desire for justice to be reinstated in the lives of these brothers-become-scoundrels. Did they repent, or even regret, what they had done to him—their own flesh and blood?

And what had they reported back to their father, Jacob, after their hateful betrayal? Over the years, did Jacob ever learn that his son had been sold like so much wheat to Ishmaelite traders for twenty pieces of silver? While Joseph was absolutely convinced that God had led him step by step to Egypt and had brought him to his considerable power, his brothers' treachery and deceitfulness were separate issues for him. Should not they be required somehow to pay for their contrived crime? Joseph struggled with how he should reveal himself to them, in light of what they had done to him. Meanwhile his brothers stood before him full of anxiety, nervously awaiting a highly uncertain outcome.

Joseph's substantial preoccupation about all this was not to be the means of his reconciliation to his brothers. All of his emotions suddenly poured out uncontrollably like the bursting of a dam. He cried so loudly and forcefully that the brothers stood in shock, not understanding at all why this head of state before them was so consumed with emotion. Joseph, knowing only that this was going to be a deeply personal family matter, composed himself enough to order all of the palace attendants out of the room. They had nearly run from the room—perplexed and frightened by the bizarre behavior of their commanding officer. But no more perplexed than these strangers from Canaan! Now alone with only his brothers, Joseph again cried so loudly that the palace personnel in adjoining rooms could hear him.

Long minutes later, Joseph was composed enough to say more. "I am your brother Joseph, the one you sold into Egypt!" (Gen. 45:4). And then, looking into Benjamin's eyes, he asked in a quieter voice, "Is my father still living?" But none of his brothers were able to answer him—not even Benjamin. They were all in shock, like men frozen. They had heard his words in this otherwise quiet room, but they could not believe or even understand what they were hearing. First, he was now talking in their language without an interpreter. Even more confounding, he referred to himself as Joseph, also the name of their brother, but surely he had died years ago. And worst of all, they were all so terrified by his authority and power that they were unable to think through any of it.

Joseph could not help but be aware of their frightened looks. All of Joseph's anger and inclination to retaliate in some way dissipated in those moments. All he wanted to do for his brothers was to relieve them of their fears, fears written clearly on their brows and seen poignantly in their eyes. He simply wanted to regain them as brothers. So gesturing with his arms, he gently encouraged them to step toward him, to be a family again. "Come close to me" (Gen. 45:4). The words dispelled some of their fears, and with some lingering uneasiness they inched closer to him.

The memory of Joseph had been all but lost in the minds of these brothers, for they could not bear to think of their despicable act all those years ago. When Joseph offered them a full pardon in the kindest of words, his forgiveness seemed like a healing balm on old, untreated wounds. With his hand gently laid on Benjamin's shoulder, Joseph explained to them, "I am your brother Joseph, the one you sold into Egypt! And now, do not be distressed and do not be angry with yourselves for selling me here, because it was to save lives that God sent me ahead of you"(Gen. 45:4–5). The grave lines on their faces began to melt away little by little as his brothers listened. A huge burden lifted from their hearts as they took in Joseph's merciful words. Joseph continued patiently to bring them on board. "For two years now there has been famine in the land and for the next five years there will be no plowing or reaping" (Gen. 45:6). Then Joseph, looking at their stunned faces, said it all a second time to be sure they understood, "But God sent me ahead of you to preserve for you a remnant on earth and to spare your lives by a great deliverance" (Gen. 45:7). As Joseph spoke to them, they came more and more to see the familiar features of their brother's face, albeit now considerably matured.

It was an experience they would never forget! Their treachery, fueled by a deep jealousy of this "favorite son" of Jacob, had been redirected by God to fulfill his own vast purposes and to save thousands of lives. They would never forget how Joseph had absolved them of all self-hatred and given them a new integrity through his gracious words. "So then it was not you who sent me here, but God. He made me father to Pharaoh, lord of his entire household and ruler of all Egypt" (Gen. 45:8). His words could not have been more generous, and his modesty amazed them.

Joseph, feeling the acceptance of his brothers, playfully seized Benjamin by the shoulders and shook him with delight, smiling as he spoke. "You *can* see . . . that it is really I who am speaking to you!" (Gen. 45:12). And then to Benjamin's surprise and delight, Joseph threw his arms around him. And both men wept as Joseph held his brother protectively. Then, to their surprise, Joseph solidly embraced and kissed each of his brothers and cried over them. These hugs were offered with such feeling that they more than confirmed the mercy and forgiveness of Joseph's words. Only then could his brothers begin to collect their thoughts and engage in conversation with him. It would be several more minutes before these brothers felt assured that their reconciliation with Joseph had complete integrity, and they could begin to enjoy what God had provided. Then they could laugh with one another more freely than ever before.

INTERPRETING

What is biblical forgiveness? Once we understand what the Bible means by forgiveness, and in particular what Jesus taught about forgiveness, we can then try to understand how to be forgiving people in the context of our marriages. Forgiveness is a very important process because, left undone, neglected, or ignored, personal relationships can quickly stagnate, suffer, or sour.

Forgiveness is one of the most misunderstood aspects of our Christian calling. Therefore, our attention to the scriptural understanding of forgiveness is vitally important, since many Christians presume to know what forgiveness is, yet fail to see the rich depth and full power of the forgiveness God freely offers to all of us and, equally important, the forgiveness he so strongly urges us to faithfully practice with one another.

Several years ago a man called me and said he had to talk to someone about his marriage. We got together, and he shared with me his discouraging, disheartening, and devastating experience. He had been married fourteen years, but the love the couple had for one another was "just about dead," a phrase he used more than once. They remained married only because they both felt it was wrong to divorce and because they did not have the financial means to do so without considerable sacrifice. I asked him what had happened. As a young man, after just six months of marriage and with his young wife's approval and support, he had enlisted in the Army. He served two years in Vietnam. While he was there, he had a three-day affair with a Vietnamese woman and had become intimately involved with her. Fortunately, he came to his senses, and by mutual consent they parted, never to see each other again.

When he came home from the war, he could not bring himself to share his infidelity with his wife. But after some eighteen months of carrying the burden of his secret, he decided to confess honestly to his wife what had happened, asking her to forgive him for succumbing to the temptation and assuring her that it was nothing more than a physical attraction that had caused his failure. His wife responded with intense feelings of anger. She felt betrayed and deeply hurt. She told him he had no right to do what he had done, and for the next several days would not allow him to touch her. Not even casually.

They could never talk freely with one another after that. He felt that they would gradually work it out and at some point continue on with a normal marriage, but that had never happened. For nearly eleven years she had refused to forgive her husband, even though he had finally found the courage to share honestly his weakness and feelings of guilt. He admitted that his marriage was only a shell of a marriage. They were merely coexisting in the same house and he had lost all hope of the two of them ever being reconciled. Without faith to give him strength and guidance, and without a Christian community to give them support and prayer, he was now feeling suicidal and needed understanding, reassurance, and advice.

What a tragedy! How different their life would have been if his wife could have eventually offered the spectacular gift of forgiveness, along with all the healing that it brings. Please understand, I am not taking the side of the husband and would have definitely benefited by hearing the wife's story. My point is that the follower of Christ has a remarkable resource for such tough situations—the way of love and forgiveness that Jesus' life exemplified.

God's gracious forgiveness of our sins is a beautiful blessing when we consider the hope and healing that it brings to our hearts and lives. When we consider offering a similarly gracious forgiveness to someone who has deeply hurt *us,* we sometimes conclude very quickly that it is not appropriate to do so, that it could be misunderstood as a weakness, or that there is an insufficient amount of remorse or apology expressed by the offending party.

The Gift of Joseph's Forgiveness to His Brothers

We need to take a close look at Joseph's forgiveness of his brothers because the sin they committed against him was appalling, deliberate, hateful, and blatant. Yet the Bible as a whole seems to be saying to us with a consistent voice: *There is no sin so hurtful, or so hateful, or so harrowing that it is unfit for God's pardon, or our forgiveness.* The question I am raising for the marital relationship is this. How much must we forgive? And how much does God want us to forgive? Exactly where does our responsibility end and the offending party's responsibility begin?

The experience of Joseph's forgiveness of his brothers is one of the best biblical illustrations of a man's complete and full forgiveness of a deliberate and appalling sin. Joseph's brothers had very nearly murdered him. Had it not been for Reuben's intervention, Joseph probably would have died under an angry and deadly assault by several of his brothers. Reuben, as one brother who was not inclined to such ruthlessness, had quickly worked out a more merciful strategy. He wanted to appease his brothers' anger by having Joseph thrown into a cistern and then hoped that his brothers would cool down. Then he could come back to rescue Joseph and safely bring him home.

That strategy was axed the moment the brothers saw on the horizon a caravan of Ishmaelite slave traders who would pay a substantial price for Joseph. They would then re-sell him on Egypt's slave market for a profit. As a consequence, Joseph ended up with a lot of hatred and cruelty to forgive because he likely heard enough of their remarks to know that his brothers were at first of a mind to kill him outright. They were relenting only because the opportunity to sell him into slavery seemed to involve less guilt for them, and, of course, there was some incentive in the monetary gain. But for Joseph, now conscious of the deep hatred of his brothers and their treacherous cruelty, the pain and suffering would be multiplied many times over as he carried this burden in his heart year after year.

Forgiving such a devious act, especially one committed by family members, is not an easy task. It certainly did not come easily for Joseph. The next time Joseph would see his brothers would be more than a decade later when he would be prime minister of Egypt. At that time, Joseph would choose to remain unknown to them, expressing his anger and resentment by taunting them in different ways.

First, he held all of them in prison for three days after threatening to hold them indefinitely as hostages (see Gen. 42:14–17). Then changing his mind, Joseph held only Simeon hostage and ordered the others to bring Benjamin back to Egypt (see Gen. 42:18–24). He also secretly put their money (the payment for the grain) back in their sacks to make them believe they were being set up for thievery, and, if caught, would probably be subject to prison (see Gen. 42:25–28). Finally, Joseph planted his own silver cup in Benjamin's bag of grain, again seen by his brothers as a setup to accuse them of stealing (see Gen. 44:1–2). Under such circumstances, they could be arrested and thrown into a dungeon where offenders were frequently left to die, forgotten by their accusers. So we can hardly say that Joseph was a prototype of Christ, as he is often depicted.

Joseph struggled long and hard with his feelings of anger and revenge. His desire for retaliation was immense. As the governor of Egypt, Joseph toyed with his brothers for at least two years (whenever they came down to Egypt for grain) and all of his malicious actions were as deliberately and intentionally planned as the crime his brothers had committed against him thirteen years earlier. Joseph apparently wanted his brothers to feel the same pain and anxiety they had caused him. While we can applaud Joseph for ultimately forgiving his brothers unconditionally and tearfully embracing them, we need to be aware that their beautiful and thorough-going reconciliation was preceded by many months of intense emotional struggle on Joseph's part before he could at last overlook their flagrant act.

There are other accounts of serious sins in the Scriptures that eventually conclude with the injured party offering forgiveness. David more than once narrowly escaped with his life when King Saul, in a rage, attempted to take David's life at close range with a spear (see 1 Sam. 18:10–11, 19:9–10). Yet when David had the power to take Saul's life, he refused to do so and appears to have somehow forgiven Saul for his wild rampages of anger, jealousy, and violence (see 1 Samuel 24 for a detailed recounting of this experience involving Saul and David). This is due in part to David's respect for the office of king, seen by him as anointed of God.

And yet, ironically, David himself is ultimately found guilty of committing adultery with Bathsheba and then, in a desperate attempt to conceal his sins, he deliberately sets up her husband, Uriah, on the field of battle so that he dies (see 2 Sam. 11). It was an especially devious cover-up since Uriah was one of his best commanders and had been constantly faithful to King David. Nevertheless, there comes eventually, thanks to the faithful prophet Nathan, the day when David's terrible secret is brought out in the open, prompting David's remorse for his conduct, and ultimately, God's gracious forgiveness of his appalling sins—sins that included deceitfulness, adultery, murder, and the grave misuse of his power as the king of Israel (see 2 Sam. 12:1–25).

In the New Testament we have the life of Saul of Tarsus, who is graphically described as a persecutor "breathing out murderous threats against the Lord's disciples" (Acts 9:1). Indeed, Saul was standing with those who stoned Stephen, the first Christian martyr, "giving approval to his death" (Acts 8:1). We are also told in Acts 8:2–3 that "Saul began to destroy the church. Going from house to house, he dragged off men and women and put them in prison." Nevertheless, Jesus dramatically appeared before Saul on a road near Damascus and began to prepare him for one of the most extensive church-building efforts in the history of Christianity (see Acts 9:1–15). No wonder the renamed *Paul* would later say, "Christ Jesus came into the world to save sinners—of whom I am the worst" (1 Tim. 1:15). Yet Paul saw his life as redeemed by Christ and forgiven. "Even though I was once a blasphemer and a persecutor and a violent man, I was shown mercy because I acted in ignorance and unbelief. The grace of our Lord was poured out on me abundantly, along with the faith and love that are in Christ Jesus" (1 Tim. 1:13–14).

There appears to be no instance in Scripture where you can point to a terrible and extremely devious sin that ultimately could *not* be forgiven. Everywhere we turn, the pages of Scripture teach us that there is no sin so grievous or so insidious or so enormous that it cannot be forgiven by the heart of God. In each case, the very modest capacity of people to forgive may require of them a long struggle before total forgiveness becomes possible. The message of God is that we need to learn somehow, someday, some way to forgive totally any who hurts us—even to the extreme of murder. Stephen, the first martyr of the Christian faith, epitomized the ideal expression of biblical forgiveness. As he was falling to the ground beneath a hail of heavy stones beating every part of his body, he offered his unforgettable testimony to the power of love and forgiveness over hatred and evil when, with his final breaths, he said, "Lord, do not hold this sin against them" (Acts 7:60). Such is the extent and fullness of God's amazing, unconditional, and all-encompassing forgiveness.

The Unhesitating Forgiveness of Jesus

Jesus' forgiveness takes us well beyond any human capacity to demonstrate this virtue. For starters, consider the breadth and depth of his forgiveness as he suffered the incomparable cruelty of crucifixion. The gospel writer Luke describes the crucifixion in such a way that one gets the impression Jesus expressed his forgiveness just as the three crosses were being lifted into place with the aid of ropes. "Two other men, both criminals, were also led out with him to be executed. When they came to the place called the Skull, there they crucified him, along with the criminals—one on his right, the other on his left. Jesus said, 'Father, forgive them, for they do not know what they are doing'" (Luke 23:32–34). Even as the soldiers raised his cross and dropped it into its stone socket, Jesus was already asking the Father to forgive them for causing his terrible suffering.

Just imagine! Jesus immediately and unhesitatingly forgives them on the grounds that they did not have the faintest idea what they were doing. Their harsh duties as Roman soldiers had apparently hardened them to such a degree that they no longer grasped the harsh inhumanity of the military orders they carried out. Note how swiftly the forgiveness comes. The nails were still like fire burning his flesh at four profusely bleeding sites. The numbness had not begun to blunt the excruciating pain, yet Jesus without hesitation manages to gasp out his words of forgiveness, absolutely absolving their guilt. No words of judgment, no pleadings for justice from the Father, no grim and angry bitterness, no threats of retribution!

Biblical scholars who have carefully examined Jesus' "last words" have tried to define the particular persons Jesus was including in the pronoun *them.* "Father, forgive *them*" (Luke 23:34). Is Jesus referring to the Sanhedrin, who had arrested him in the night and set him up for crucifixion by the Roman military by manipulating a series of night trials, false witnesses, and a coached crowd at Pilate's palace? Or is Jesus simply referring to the Roman soldiers assigned to this watch, with orders to crucify three men, Jesus being one of the three? Jesus was never careless with words, yet here he offers no precise definition about exactly who he is forgiving. And so the plural pronoun *them* (or *they*) must include anyone and everyone who had a part in putting him on the cross. What generosity and grace Christ shows! Many persons had been involved in this torturous act of execution: torchbearers who made the night arrest in Gethsemane; all the false witnesses who accepted bribes for their lies; rulers such as Pilate and Herod, who failed to use their power to protect an innocent party; and the squad of soldiers, who were under orders to oversee three executions. Are all such persons included in his appeal to the Father that *they* be forgiven? If so, what a sublime and stellar forgiveness Christ unhesitatingly offers!

Those of us who see Jesus as the epitome of human values and earnestly desire to reach toward his elegant stature, must pause to ask ourselves how much, if any, of this sublime quality has been found breathing in us and giving out its life. Suppose that a close relative opposed the choice you made in marriage and on more than one occasion had brought up things from your husband's past that misrepresented the man he was now. Could you graciously forgive that relative on the grounds that he did not know what he was doing? Or suppose your daughter backed her car out of your driveway and struck your poodle—injuring the animal so badly that it had to be put to sleep. Could you forgive her on the grounds that she simply did not realize what she was doing? Or consider one more situation. Let us suppose that your husband succumbed one evening to the sexual advances of a younger woman at his workplace at a time in your marriage when things were already overwhelming (e.g., three children to raise, a part-time job that was highly stressful, etc.), could you forgive him solely on the basis that he really had no clue how much this would hurt you?

And if you could, through prayer, actually practice the forgiveness and graciousness of Christ in any one of these situations, how long would it take you to set your spouse completely free from any and all condemnation and resentment on your part? How many weeks or months would it take you to be a loving spouse who was no longer holding onto even the slightest resentfulness or anger? Or would it take you years to deal with these hurts, as in Joseph's case?

The forgiveness that Jesus offers is remarkable because it is *undeserved, unhesitating,* and *unconditional.* Jesus does not wait until he is clear of the worst of his pain and has a clearer mind to assess the situation. He does not wait until his tormentors first offer some form of apology or express some remorse. Jesus does not wait until some other time in the day when he would hopefully be "in the mood." Rather, he offers his forgiveness immediately and generously, while he is experiencing the sheer terror of crucifixion at its worst—during the first terrifying minutes.

Dare we act with Christ's bold forgiveness in those hurtful situations in our marriage? Many a spouse, experiencing a deep hurt, sets into motion the divorce process and never looks back. Only those who understand the bounteous extent of Christ's forgiveness can understand its miraculous power to bring healing and new life into an otherwise shipwrecked marriage.

We will discuss the humility of Christ in chapter eleven, and how essential that quality is in a healthy marriage. Humility is also absolutely needed in the spouse who is considering this extraordinary way of dealing with a terrible hurt that the world can only see as unforgiveable—to be "resolved" only in divorce. Under such circumstances, divorce may be to some degree personally satisfying to the person who is hurt, in terms of the justice that it personally achieves. The offender at least "pays" for his or her offense. But that is hardly the life-giving gift that Christ's forgiveness can bestow so beautifully, freely restoring and wondrously recreating the gift of love, perhaps at a deeper level than ever before experienced throughout the marriage. But for too many, our stubbornness, willfulness, and even self-righteousness may be just as strong and antagonistic as our mate's hurtful action, moral failure, or thoughtless indulgence.

I am not suggesting that an abused spouse should remain in a dangerous situation. Forgiveness does not require a victim of physical or verbal abuse to remain in a situation where nothing seems to have changed in the heart and mind of the abuser. Rather, I am contending that Jesus has given us a powerful resource that can often soften a spouse's heart and end the repetitive hurtfulness, giving a fresh start to the marriage—a blank page on which we can prayerfully learn how to say "I love you" again.

In conclusion, one can summarize the biblical perspective something like this: *there is no sin so hurtful or so hateful or so harrowing that it is beyond God's mercy, or even beyond our personal forgiveness as followers of Christ.* If that is what we conclude about the biblical understanding of forgiveness, our next task is to examine our own practice of forgiveness in marriage. Spiritually, are we stretching to reach toward Christ's imposing way of forgiveness, or possibly finding it easier to rationalize, excuse, or justify why, in some particular instance, or with some particular person, we are content to withhold the gift of forgiveness.

INTEGRATING

First, let us consider what you may be dealing with in your marriage. What is it that you need to forgive? We have already touched upon the more difficult situations that may remain unforgiven in a marital relationship, such as an unfaithful partner. But most of us are probably struggling with issues that are far less commanding, yet still causing hurt, irritation, frustration, resentment, and even anger. Are any of these scenarios relevant to your situation?

- Your husband never leaves the bathroom in an attractive and reasonably clean condition. Towels may be left on the floor, the toilet seat up, the sink water-soaked, the toothpaste uncapped, etc.
- Your wife spends too much time (in your view) reading romantic novels and watching celebrity shows to keep up with the family's basic needs—such as meals and laundry.
- Your spouse is almost always late for social events with friends and family gatherings and seems not to care about how embarrassed you feel about this thoughtless and annoying habit.
- Your husband seems to view football (or, insert his favorite sport here) as a priority over cutting the lawn or doing a home repair, rather than as a reward for getting such necessary work completed.
- Your spouse almost never takes the time to enter checkbook transactions properly, misplaces receipts from ATMs, and is generally careless about financial transactions, thereby causing unnecessary or avoidable penalty fees by the bank.

You may not have to deal with the intense anger and desire for retaliation caused by an extramarital affair, but you are left to deal with a simmering anger or smoldering frustration that is wearing on your relationship. Such irritations certainly do not bring energy, vitality, excitement, and joy to a marriage. What do we do with these unwanted feelings when all of our entreaties have somehow fallen on deaf ears for years? If change in your partner is not possible, what, if anything, can you do?

For me, the simple answer is genuine, prayerfully gathered forgiveness. Whether the act is a single, shocking deed that makes the newspapers, or a careless, thoughtless habit that is acted out almost daily, peace comes only through the healing power of forgiveness. If unfaithfulness can be forgiven, surely thoughtlessness or a lack of consideration can be forgiven! And so, Mark writes to the world these all-encompassing, all-embracing words of Jesus: "Therefore I tell you, whatever you ask for in prayer, believe that you have received it, and it will be yours. And when you stand praying, *if you hold anything against anyone,* forgive him, so that your Father in heaven may forgive you your sins" (Mark 11:24–25, emphasis mine). I believe that the "anything" mentioned above includes such repetitive offences as sloppiness, thoughtless habits, a lack of responsibility, and perpetual lateness.

You may be asking, how does such forgiveness help? It helps me because it sets me free of all my feelings of frustration and irritation and enables me fully to love the person again. Have you ever noticed how such irritations—which almost always grate on us in the privacy of our home, turning our skies gray—when brought out into our circle of close friends, possibly over dinner at a restaurant, often result in sensitive teasing, harmless banter, and the release of delightful laughter rather than accusation or anger, nagging, or nastiness.

Sensitive friends simply love us despite all of our crazy baggage and will not take seriously the raised toilet seat, the ATM receipt dropped in the rain, or the un-manicured lawn. They will create fun and laughter for everyone as they tease and play with the topic of conversation at hand, even to the point of graciously sharing their own idiosyncrasies and light stories. Instead of frustration, we all have fun, the kind of wholesome fun that does not single out one particular person, causing him or her to feel put down in front of others, but a gentle sharing of those times when we had no recourse but to laugh at ourselves. It may even be remembered as one of the highlights of the evening, to be shared in other settings in the days ahead.

None of our friends would ever even think to say formally, "Norm, we forgive you for losing your ATM receipts." But that is precisely what is assumed or implied. They love you fully for other qualities that are far more significant than forgetting a raised toilet seat, namely your faithful friendship through the years, or the night you came to their aid when their basement flooded, or your loving support for them when their son committed suicide.

When we are truly set free from our simmering anger, we can approach our spouse with a teasing comment rather than a provoked voice. Instead of, "Harold, you have made an absolute mess of our bathroom again, and I just cleaned it yesterday!" try, "Harold darling, it truly baffles me how you can get this much water on the counter and floor without a fire hose!" If it does not cause him one day to towel up with a smile some of the water, at least your life will be lifted to a greater inward joy and peace. In the Lord's Prayer, it says, "Forgive us our debts, as we also have forgiven our debtors" (Matt. 6:12). I used to believe that *debts* (plural) simply referred to our varied sins. I now believe that it *also* refers to the thoughtless aggravations that are repeated many times over.

How Biblical Forgiveness Works

The fullness of biblical forgiveness will not be experienced very often, simply because it is so *all-encompassing*, is *freely* given, and involves *no exceptions.* By contrast, many of us find some reason to excuse ourselves from offering the same gracious forgiveness offered to us through the grace of Jesus Christ. Consider these three characteristics of biblical forgiveness as you prayerfully reflect on how you're going to process your own hurt(s).

Biblical Forgiveness is Unconditional: The forgiveness that Christ teaches us to practice has no conditions laid out for us to fulfill before our forgiveness is operative. Christ was in the very process of painfully dying, yet he offered an unqualified forgiveness to his tormentors. When the Scriptures speak about forgiveness, they do not encourage us to offer forgiveness and then name several conditions that must first be met by the offender. Jesus prays from the cross, "Father, forgive them, for they do not know what they are doing" (Luke 23:34). He does not pray, "Father, forgive them when they come to their senses and feel some remorse for having taken my life."

Repetitive Sinning Is to Be Repeatedly Forgiven: Simon Peter once asked Jesus a question about how many times he was personally bound to forgive an offender. "Lord, how many times shall I forgive my brother when he sins against me?" (Matt. 18:21). Peter then threw in his best guess, which he likely felt was quite generous: "Up to seven times?" (Matt. 18:21). And Jesus' answer had to startle, and even shock, the disciples. "I tell you, not seven times, but seventy-seven times" (Matt. 18:22). That moves the bar up considerably! Jesus of course means something like this. "Do not waste your time counting—*just make forgiveness your permanent and unwavering lifestyle.*" This is a very important concept, because many of the sins committed against us are repetitive, such as the husband who spends so much time fishing or golfing on the weekends that he fails to fulfill his role as husband and/or father, and further burdens his wife with the important tasks of parenting, homemaking, etc.

It Matters Not Whether the Offense Is Committed Unconsciously, or Is Deliberately Contrived: I take longer to forgive offenses and hurts that I feel have been deliberately and intentionally contrived. When Joseph's brothers sold him into slavery, it was maliciously planned and done with a conscious awareness. It was much more difficult for Joseph to deal with than forgiving them for not having sufficient courage or skill to protect him when some attacking party caught them by surprise and in the process captured Joseph and sold him into slavery. It does not matter at all whether the offense was done to us consciously or unconsciously, unapologetically or with remorse, intentionally or unknowingly, accidentally or even accompanied with ridicule—the Scriptures see none of this as an excuse or exception. The person who has hurt you may even feel that he has nothing to apologize for—that your hurt is simply imagined. You would still be wise to forgive, and thereby be "released" of the entire situation. As a friend of mine aptly stated, think of it as a gift you give yourself.

Whatever the sin, however it was performed, the Scriptures teach us to find the path of wholehearted, unqualified forgiveness. The Lord is our example. "Praise the LORD, O my soul, and forget not all his benefits—who forgives *all your sins* and heals all your diseases" (Ps. 103:2–4, emphasis mine). There is nothing complicated about the concept of biblical forgiveness. When the apostle Paul writes to the church at Ephesus, he says, "Get rid of *all* bitterness, rage and anger, brawling and slander, along with *every* form of malice. Be kind and compassionate to one another, *forgiving each other,* just as in Christ God forgave you" (Eph. 4:31–32, emphasis mine). The Scriptures offer no exceptions, not one!

A Word of Encouragement

I would be less than honest if I suggested that Jesus' approach to forgiveness is easy. Of all the qualities and attitudes needed to have a healthy and joyous marriage, I would venture to say that forgiveness—as taught and practiced by our Lord—is the most challenging of all, probably because it clashes with our egos. We want to have some control over those who hurt us, and Jesus' forgiveness absolves them of all guilt, gives them a fresh beginning, and sets them absolutely free. Many of us are not humble enough to walk in that direction. How many stories or testimonies have you heard from Christian married couples, in which the theme is that their struggling relationship became vitalized as a result of intentionally learning to be as totally forgiving toward each other as Jesus has been with us?

Moreover, Christian preachers and teachers have not been diligent enough in helping the Christian community clearly understand the real nature of biblical forgiveness. Pastors often preach sermons on forgiveness but assume the person in the pew has an accurate biblical understanding of the term. *In fact, if we are totally honest, we preachers (myself included) have too often not understood biblical forgiveness ourselves.* And when we are not clear about how something works, especially expectations that are going to require something substantial of us, we are not going to be able to step into it with a strong conviction and with a willingness to entertain a sizable risk.

If I have only a vague understanding of God's way of forgiveness, real reconciliation is simply not going to happen. But if I am convinced through God's Word that forgiveness has very specific and definable characteristics that have been clearly portrayed in Jesus' life (for example, his forgiveness is unconditional, unhesitating, etc.), I am much more able to make an unwavering decision to personally live it out. If you still have some hesitation, begin with something small, like the kids' failure to hang up their coats (assuming that frustrates or angers you). Test out the biblical principles to see if they actually give you greater peace and a greater freedom in which to lovingly teach your children to do their part of "keeping house" by hanging up their coats in the place provided. After praying about it for several days (or whatever time you need), see if you become more relaxed, and even playful, in the way you meet them at the front door after school. "Oh, no, you don't—those coats deserve to be lovingly placed on a hanger, because I happen to know they've been thrown around enough today—especially Erica's coat! Yes, even coats have rights! *To the closet—march!*"

Again, I cannot stress enough how important it is for us to be "prayed up"—did you *honestly* take a minute or so during the day to sit down at the kitchen table or on your lunch break at work and pray about this one problem—I mean, really asking God to set you free of the I-feel-ready-to-murder-someone attitude! Without God's help and his spirit of love, I doubt that you can be the special kind of loving mom or dad, or the Christlike husband or wife that you want to be. If that sounds simplistic, remember that God wants all of us to live a life that is chock-full of the fruit of his Spirit, which is "love, joy, peace, patience, kindness, goodness, faithfulness, gentleness and self-control" (Gal. 5:22–23). That's the direction God wants to see us moving, and it can come only through the help of the Holy Spirit. It will happen in your life when you trust Jesus' words and desire to honor him by following his way without compromise.

A Prayer

Lord of life, thanks for your forgiveness—a forgiveness which is surprisingly unconditional and remarkably unhesitating—a forgiveness which includes sins great and small. Now that I understand better the way your forgiveness works, I desire to learn how to live that out in my marriage, so that our love for each other will no longer feel suffocated in the polluted air of frustration, resentment, and repressed anger. I confess that I have never been very good at forgiveness and probably find it to be one of the more difficult things to practice. But today, knowing that it is your desire for me, please grant me your help and your spirit of love so that your gracious forgiveness becomes a major characteristic in my life, and in every day of our marriage. I pray, trusting in Jesus for the courage to change. Amen.

Three Questions

1. What annoys, irritates, or hurts you the most in your relationship with your spouse? In that one area, do you feel ready to deal with it in the spirit of Jesus' love? Are you willing to pray your way through it, to the end that your husband/wife may hopefully understand the fullness of your forgiveness, and both of you experience a greater freedom and joy in each other?

2. What aspect of Jesus' forgiveness most amazes you? If you were humbly and sincerely to practice that aspect of forgiveness, would your husband/wife also be amazed?

3. Do you believe that Christ's understanding of forgiveness could bring a new vitality and real healing to your marriage? Why is healing potentially an outcome of biblical forgiveness?

INSIGHTS

"God has a big eraser."

—Billy Zeoli

"I can forgive, but I cannot forget," is only another way of saying, "I will not forgive." Forgiveness ought to be like a cancelled note— torn in two and burned up so it never can be shown against one.

—Henry Ward Beecher

Forgiveness is an act of the will, and the will can function regardless of the temperature of the heart.

—Corrie ten Boom

I will not permit any man to narrow and degrade my soul by making me hate him.

—Booker T. Washington

He who forgives ends the quarrel.

—African Proverb

Forgive us our debts, as we also have forgiven our debtors.

—The Lord's Prayer

A happy marriage is the union of two good forgivers.

—Robert Quillen

For if you forgive men when they sin against you, your heavenly Father will also forgive you. But if you do not forgive men their sins, your Father will not forgive you your sins.

—Jesus (Matt. 6:14–15)

Everyone says forgiveness is a lovely idea, until they have something to forgive.

—C. S. Lewis

Humanity is never so beautiful as when praying for forgiveness or else forgiving another.

—Jean Paul Richter

There are three things that are too amazing for me, four that I do not understand: the way of an eagle in the sky, the way of a snake on a rock, the way of a ship on the high seas, and the way of a man with a maiden.

—Prov. 30:18–19

LOVE AND SEXUALITY—
LET'S TALK!

INTERPERSONAL

Have you ever received a gift that was so special, so unique, and so beautiful that there was no way to compare it with any others? When Joanne and I were in our late teens, we were enjoying the friendship of other youth at our church and growing in our faith—thanks to our devoted adult leadership. We were senior high youth who were approaching graduation when a man named Herman Wollenweber, a dedicated Christian with a passion for the poor, asked if we would consider leading a children's ministry in Baltimore's waterfront ghetto, one of the city's worst areas. After talking it over and praying about it, we were convinced that God wanted us to go for it.

I had some art training, so we decided to use illustrations to teach these elementary age children the stories of the Bible that we ourselves had learned in church school. While I quickly sketched the biblical story with colored chalk, Joanne taught them from the same account. The kids loved these stories and sat quietly and attentively, at times spellbound.

The first evening we did this, several of the children came to us to ask if they could take the "pit-chur" home. So we would spray the chalk drawing with fixative, roll it up on a cardboard core, and present it to a different child each week. The kids were thrilled! We later discovered, when visiting a couple of their homes one evening, that the mom or dad had allowed the kids to tape these large unframed sketches to the walls of their homes! In one case, the sketch covered an especially bad area of the child's bedroom wall where the plaster had fallen away from the now exposed wooden batten.

After two years of leading this Friday night ministry, we felt God's direction to prepare for full-time pastoral ministry. This involved seven years of higher education. When we had to move for this purpose, we also had to say farewell to these children, who had so captured our hearts. We did not look forward to our last evening together, because we knew how much we would miss them, along with the possibility we might never see them again.

On our final evening we had some special treats and games for them and our usual chalk talk, this final one on Jesus' resurrection. We wanted to leave with them the hope that God gives to all of us. At the end of the evening after our closing prayer, one of the girls came forward shyly and presented us with a gift wrapped in a lunch bag, tied at the top with a string for a bow. The child handed the gift to Joanne, saying timidly, "Gonna miss you." She was on the verge of crying and so were we. We opened the bag, carefully unveiling a small potted petunia, which we later learned was purchased with pennies and nickels collected by the children.

The petunia was visibly drooped and dying, as it had probably been wrapped for several hours, or even the day before! But of the many gifts that we have received over the years, that gift still stands out as one of the most precious we ever received. It was a unique, one-of-a-kind gift—a beautiful expression of the children's love for us!

So too, of all the earthly gifts we have received from our heavenly Father, and they are more than we could ever name or number, one of the most remarkable and incomparable is the gift God gave to us as husband and wife, the gift of our sexuality, a beautiful expression of his great love for us. And it still amazes me that God would trust us with such a thrilling gift—a gift with the awesome power of enabling one other very special person to experience an almost indescribable joy and intense pleasure! It remains for me a constant reminder of just how much Christ cherishes us—entrusting us with this wondrous gift that we in turn can lovingly give to each other—again and again and again!

INSPIRING

[First, the words offered by the wife, about her husband.]

My lover is radiant and ruddy, outstanding among ten thousand. His head is purest gold; his hair is wavy and black as a raven. His eyes are like doves by the water streams, washed in milk, mounted like jewels. His cheeks are like beds of spice yielding perfume. His lips are like lilies dripping with myrrh. His arms are rods of gold set with chrysolite. His body is like polished ivory decorated with sapphires. His legs are pillars of marble set on bases of pure gold. His appearance is like Lebanon, choice as its cedars. His mouth is sweetness itself; he is altogether lovely. This is my lover, this my friend, O daughters of Jerusalem.

—Song of Songs 5:10–16

[Next, the words offered by the husband, about his wife.]

How beautiful your sandaled feet, O prince's daughter! Your graceful legs are like jewels, the work of a craftsman's hands. Your navel is a rounded goblet that never lacks blended wine.

Your waist is a mound of wheat encircled by lilies. Your breasts are like two fawns, twins of a gazelle. Your neck is like an ivory tower. Your eyes are the pools of Heshbon by the gate of Bath Rabbim. Your nose is like the tower of Lebanon looking toward Damascus. Your head crowns you like Mount Carmel. Your hair is like royal tapestry; the king is held captive by its tresses.

How beautiful you are and how pleasing, O love, with your delights! Your stature is like that of the palm, and your breasts like clusters of fruit. I said, "I will climb the palm tree; I will take hold of its fruit." May your breasts be like the clusters of the vine, the fragrance of your breath like apples, and your mouth like the best wine.

—Song of Songs 7:1–9

[The section below is the woman's response]

May the wine go straight to my lover, flowing gently over lips and teeth. I belong to my lover, and his desire is for me. Come, my lover, let us go to the countryside, let us spend the night in the villages. Let us go early to the vineyards to see if the vines have budded, if their blossoms have opened, and if the pomegranates are in bloom—there I will give you my love. The mandrakes send out their fragrance, and at our door is every delicacy, both new and old, that I have stored up for you, my lover.

—Song of Songs 7:9–13

IMAGINING

(Dedicated to my wife, Joanne, who has helped me immeasurably to understand and enjoy the many aspects of love!)

The Many Aspects of Love

Love sometimes just happens
Like the evening I first met you,
Finally mustering the courage to approach you for the last dance.
I still remember your flashing blue eyes
Sparkling with life!
Love enjoys the moment.
Love is at times relaxed and unhurried
Like a young plant imperceptibly growing,
Or soup simmering slowly.
We'd meet after school, nothing special planned,
Except to be together.
What all did we find to talk about so comfortably,
So incessantly?
We'd stop at the corner drug store for a fountain soda
And spend over an hour sipping it
And sharing the stories of our lives.
And as we gradually learned about each other,

We were getting to know ourselves.
Love rests in the other.
Love takes its time.
Love is outgoing, a good mixer.
Love wants to be with people.
Love creates a circle of friends, like our Sunday night youth group—
A place for us to grow spiritually in Christ.
I recall the fun and laughter—
Races in potato sacks,
Bobbing for apples 'round Halloween,
A crazy relay carrying jiggling jelly beans on teaspoons
To their empty soda bottle destination!
We had our serious moments too—
Especially when it came our turn to lead devotions.
But we were among friends who really loved us.
They'd tell us that we did well and they meant it,
And thank us for sharing.
Afterwards, we would drive out to Bunny's for wild, super-sized
    desserts,
In cars so packed that closing the last door was often a problem.
Occasionally you were perched awkwardly on at least a part of my
    lap,
Both of us scrunched in between friends.
Not terribly romantic—but definitely fun!
Love measures its wealth in faithful friends.
Love is commitment.
We stood side by side at the front of the church,
Overflowing with people,
All very happy for us.
We promised to love one another
"As long as we both shall live."
We pledged to faithfully love one another for a lifetime
When we scarcely knew what that meant.
We held hands as prayers were offered for us,
And then placed rings on each other's fingers, endless circles of gold,
Reminders that our love was for keeps.
Then hugs and warm wishes from a steady stream of family and
    friends,
Untiring smiles on our faces

Love is a keeper.
Love makes wise choices
Like practicing forgiveness,
Refusing to criticize,
Holding your tongue,
Celebrating birthdays and holidays as a family,
Learning how to create a warm home,
Calling a friend whose heart is aching,
Faithfully worshipping God at church each Sunday,
Our hands clasped during the prayers,
And side by side singing the great hymns of our faith.
And after the benediction,
Bonding with people at the reception—
Lots of laughter,
Loads of listening,
Forging lasting friendships that would later strengthen and encourage
     us.
Love is making good choices.
Love is taking the time.
Love is sometimes a servant—
Preparing the dinner, washing the dishes,
Waxing the floor, repairing the door,
Caring for a sick child during the night,
Delivering "Meals on Wheels" together,
Taking the time to visit a grieving friend,
Or traveling a thousand miles on a bus with thirty other folks
To help the people of Mississippi rebuild their lives,
While rebuilding their hurricane-ravaged homes
Love calms our worst fears.
Love can handle the tears.
Love often rolls up its shirtsleeves.
Love does not mind the sweat.
Love volunteers.
Sometimes love seems like a miracle.
Joanne tells me that the pregnancy test is positive.
We have waited for this moment for nearly ten years!
The mystery of life being nurtured protectively inside my wife—
Tiny toes and tiny fingers forming in the darkness of her womb
She takes my hand gently one evening,

Placing it on the firm roundness of her swelling belly.
I wait a few moments for what she wants me to know.
I hold my breath and listen.
And *then*, the soft bump of a tiny foot kicking within!
"He's going to be a soccer player," I say.
The moment comes when I hold our newborn daughter for the very
    first time,
Feeling the very threshold of life trembling in my hands—
The breathtaking gift of God!
The Creator is still creating.
Love brings life.
Love is patient.
Love is faithful,
Getting up in the middle of the night,
Awakened by our infant's anxious, alarming crying
Again!
I take her warm, wrestling body gently in my arms,
Still uncontrollably sobbing.
As inexperienced parents, we troubleshoot groggily, trying this and that.
I shift her awkwardly to her mother's arms.
Rocked gently, she settles at last,
And we silently stumble back to bed,
The room already brightening with morning.
But love is strong and bears such things.
Love perseveres.
Love is patient.
Love is being there.
The phone rings around midnight on a snowy night.
The call is from a hospital maternity wing fifty miles away.
"They are letting me stay with her . . . her pains are getting close . . .
I thought you guys would like to know . . .
Yes, we are expecting eight to ten inches here . . ."
We hang up the phone and in minutes we are dressed and ready to
    go.
We are out the door like kids heading to a super-park!
We are usually sensible about snowstorms,
But this is an exception.
Snow quickly accumulates on the interstate.

Large snowflakes assault the windshield like invaders from space!
We talk to keep each other alert.
We are well repaid for our anxious trip—
Knowing our daughter was doing well and comfortably resting,
Getting to see Charis's wide open eyes already taking in life!
And seeing her twin sister, Sydney, so relaxed in her incubator
Set at mom's comfortable warmth.
Love at the first sight of our twin granddaughters!
Love is responsive.
Love is being there.
Love is sharing joys.
A dinner out with friends
An evening of laughter
Sharing our stories with those close enough to tease us
And make fun of our quirks
A story gives rise to ripples of giggling and escalates to howling!
Spontaneous responses fuel the fun.
We talk of serious matters too—
Receiving understanding and encouragement.
Love enjoys people!
Love listens.
Love casts out fear.
Love is unafraid.
We sit in the quiet of the waiting room.
Finally your name is called.
She can see you now.
"The CAT-scan shows a mass in the left breast."
She tells us almost at a whisper.
Love is my hand clasping yours . . .
And then . . . another unwanted day . . .
My neurologist is young enough to be my grandson!
He gives us the information in a gentle but straightforward manner:
"Bob, you have a movement disorder known as Parkinson's Disease."
Love is your hand clasping mine.
These uninvited, unsought, and unwanted occasions would become
      spiritual tests
To see what we have learned.
Love holds on.
Love casts out fear.

Love sometimes just happens.
Love takes its time.
Love brings life.
Love is commitment, love is a keeper.
Love makes good choices.
Love is being there.
Love is faithful.
Love at times seems like a miracle.
Love is sharing laughter.
Love perseveres.
Love listens.
Love is unafraid.
Love is holding on.
Love never ends.

INTERPRETING

The most significant thing about our sexuality as a man or woman is that *its designer and creator is God.* Because of our God-given sexuality, we are creatures who can experience the most incredible pleasures imaginable—the ecstasy of experiencing oneness as husband and wife. God is the sole origin of this exquisite experience. He gave it to us as one of his most extraordinary gifts. It is a gift so powerful that a man and woman standing on opposite sides of a room can feel a sensual attraction and desire that is nearly as tangible as a touch. God was willing to create us with that powerful built-in emotional attraction and physical desire, knowing full well the great risks involved in its potential for misuse and manipulation. God was willing to take that huge risk because he wanted to give us the priceless gift of being able to give an ecstatic experience of joy to one another within the security, stability, and strength of the marriage relationship.

Think of lovemaking as God's gift of ecstasy to both of you as a couple joined together in marriage. God has created us sexually, male and female, so that we could enjoy intimacy and freely give pleasure and joy to one another. It is not coincidental that a man enjoys looking into a woman's eyes, or casually running his fingers through her soft, lovely hair during an intimate conversation. It is not an accident of nature that a woman enjoys a man's warm smile or seeing the strong lines of his shoulders and forearms. We were made that way deliberately as a result of God's infinite creativity and thought. Along with the psalmist, I find that "the way of a man with a maiden" is "too amazing" for me to comprehend fully (Prov. 30:18–19). Think of the act of making love as the sweetest source of joy that you can give your mate.

We are so out of touch with this fundamental understanding of our sexuality as the creation of God that many of us take pride in our appearance, as if we had contributed a great deal of input, insight, and ingenuity into our body's design. The glamorous Hollywood star struts before the cameras as though he had engineered his own body. *He received it as a gift of God!* Admittedly, we have the ability and means to enhance our attractiveness with cologne and cosmetics, hairstyling and highlighting, exercise and attire. But our basic structure, shape, and sexuality come from God as his gift. He chooses the flowing form of our lips, the texture and fullness of our hair, the color and slant of our eyes. The person chosen to be Miss America can be commended for being disciplined with her workouts, restrained in terms of her diet, skillful in terms of her make-up, and tasteful in terms of her selected wardrobe. But her crown owes much more to God in terms of her genetics than to such enhancements as jewelry or fashion.

Our awareness that we have been skillfully sculptured by an infinitely creative Mind is the most important aspect of our understanding of our intelligence, sexuality, creativity, or any other aspect of our humanity. The psalmist states it with incredible clarity. "Know ye that the LORD he is God: it is he that hath made us, *and not we ourselves*" (Ps. 100:3 KJV, emphasis mine).

If Our Sexuality is God Given, It Must Be Treated with Dignity

When I was in my early teens, I spent a lot of time with two neighborhood friends. Both had the habit of using crude words I had never heard in my home, words that related largely to the male or female body. I did not have to ask their meaning, because they were used in a certain context and it became obvious what was meant. Instinctively I knew I could not adopt them because they were never used in my home. I did not, however, have a clue about why it was wrong, inappropriate speech. Using such crude language seemed to give my two friends a certain toughness, and for me, a measure of uneasiness. I noticed that such words were never used by my friends in the presence of my parents (or even the corner grocer). They were additionally cloaked in the darkness of the forbidden. I never brought the matter to my parents because I thought they might not allow me to continue in these friendships.

When I was about fifteen, my mom and dad encouraged my sister and me to check out a youth group that met in a nearby church. (We did not have one in our own church, and my parents decided to make a change that would more likely contribute to our growth in faith.) These new Christian friends, we quickly noticed, never used "street language"—even when angry. The experience was so refreshing that I felt easily drawn into these new friendships, and without really deciding to let go of my two neighborhood friends, I gradually saw less and less of them.

Of course, the reason such words are inappropriate is because they demean our bodies, which have been created by God. If we indeed believe that our bodies, including our sexuality, are the work of God's hands, then it follows that we must treat them with respect and dignity. There is biblical support for this in Song of Songs, where virtually every part of the human body is referred to openly, respectfully, and comfortably.

Each part of the male or female body is poetically described in Song of Songs (NIV) in the context of romance, marriage, and sexuality. Reference is made to the "head" (2:6; 5:2, 11; 7:5); the "hair" (4:1; 5:2, 11; 6:5; 7:5); her "tresses" (7:5); the "neck" (1:10; 4:4; 7:4); both the "left arm" and the "right arm" (2:6; 8:3, 6); the "hand" (5:4–5); the "fingers" (5:5); his "body" (5:14); the "legs" (5:15; 7:1); and "feet" (5:3 and 7:1). Song of Songs also finds beauty in the "face" (2:14); the "eyes" (4:1, 9; 5:12; 6:5; 7:4; 8:10), the "nose" (7:4); the "mouth" (1:2; 4:3; 5:16; 7:9); the "lips" (4:3, 11; 5:13; 7:9); the "temples" or forehead (4:3; 6:7); the "cheeks" (1:10; 5:13); the "teeth"

(4:2; 6:6; 7:9); the "tongue" (4:11); the "breath" (7:8); the "voice" (2:14; 8:13); and the complexion (5:10). Also included with the same openness are the "navel" (7:2); the "waist" (7:2); the "heart" (3:1–4; 4:9; 5:2, 6; 8:6); the "breasts" (1:13; 4:5; 7:3, 7–8; 8:8, 10); the woman's "stature" (7:7); and, described with three artful metaphors, the vagina, specifically of the bride, while still in her virginity (4:12).

The writer/poet is not trying to offer a complete cataloging of the anatomy of a man or woman. Rather, he is calling attention to those features of our body that have a role in the sexual experience of attraction, romance, and making love, which in turn, provide stimulation and pleasure for both partners as they touch, kiss, caress, and look upon one another.

These Lovers Warmly Affirmed Each Other

Moreover, the body's various features are beautifully described for their elegance and attractiveness in very warm and affirming personal statements by both the man and the woman as they converse with one another. The man, describing his bride, says in Song of Songs 4:1, "Your hair is like a flock of goats descending from Mount Gilead." Note that he is comparing her flowing hair to *the course of movement* of the goats as they descend down a steep hillside. The animals must take a course that is constantly swinging first to the right, then to the left, back and forth, on a course similar to the relaxed curls in the woman's long, flowing hair.

Again, he says to her, "Your teeth are like a flock of sheep just shorn, coming up from the washing. Each has its twin; not one of them is alone" (Song of Songs 4:2). Here, the man visualizes a flock of sheep, coming up out of the water, their white bodies wet and gleaming in the sunlight. As they reach the crest of the hill, all walking tightly together, they appear much like the beautiful line of white teeth seen in the bride's smile, each tooth having a corresponding "twin."

When he tells her that her lips are "like a scarlet ribbon" (Song of Songs 4:3), we can easily relate to the passionate scarlet color and the smooth sensation of touching a ribbon. He also compares her eyes to "the pools of Heshbon" (7:4), and we may imagine the sparkle of the sun's reflection in blue water. Again, he says to her on another occasion, "Your cheeks are beautiful with earrings, your neck with strings of jewels" (1:10). When he speaks of the fragrance of her breath as being like apples (7:8), we do not have to stretch very much to know that the scent is pleasant and familiar, since we have probably experienced it in our own perfumes and candles.

Their thoughts for one another come from their hearts. They are inspired by what they are seeing and experiencing. "Your neck is like the tower of David, built with elegance; on it hang a thousand shields" (Song of Songs 4:4). The tower of David, possibly made of smooth plaster walls, would have been as refreshing and inspiring a piece of architecture three millennia ago, as Frank Lloyd Wright's dramatic creations, which inspired many this past century. The hundreds of colorful and artfully adorned shields of David's legendary warriors were hung on the tower wall, ready to seize when the battle cry was sounded. What a beautiful metaphor to use to describe the elegance of the woman's neck, undoubtedly adorned with a unique and colorful necklace, perhaps made of dangling metal chips, each skillfully painted with many gleaming colors. David's tower has not survived the ages, but this reference to it assures us that its walls were likely smooth, and certainly not made of rough-hewn stone.

And finally, speaking to her on their wedding night, he says that her breasts are like two fawns, like twin fawns of a gazelle that browse among the lilies (see Song of Songs 4:5 and 7:3). Do we understand what the husband is communicating to his bride—an image familiar to him from his pastoral life? When fawns graze in a field of mature lilies, you cannot see their legs at all. The fawns forage with their heads tucked down and out of sight, so as to reach the grasses beneath the flowers. This groom is recalling the roundness of their rumps pushed up through a sea of lilies as resembling his bride's white skin, the fullness of her breasts rising above the less dramatic lines of her resting body. He sees and appreciates each aspect of her body for its beauty. No wonder he says to her more than once, "How beautiful you are, my darling! Oh, how beautiful!" (1:15; 4:1).

The woman describes her husband as "handsome" and "charming" (Song of Songs 1:16). His hair is "wavy and black as a raven" (5:11), and "his mouth is sweetness itself" (5:16). When she describes his eyes, they are "like doves by the water streams, washed in milk, mounted like jewels" (5:12). We imagine his eyes as flashing and alive with reflected light—the eye's iris like a brilliant colored jewel. When the bride tells us why she chose him to be her husband, she speaks adoringly of his strength: "His arms are rods of gold set with chrysolite" (5:14). The man's body is toned and well defined, and his forearms are deeply "cut," as they say in fitness circles. Chrysolite is a gem that comes in a variety of colors, but in this case probably refers to the golden, brownish variety of olivine. Together, the deep cuts in his muscular arms, along with his golden-brown tan, resemble "rods of gold." Both husband and wife put some thought and imagination into their affirming words.

Apparently something similar to our cologne was used by men some three thousand years ago. It must have been a turn-on then as now because the woman says to him, "My lover is to me a sachet of myrrh resting between my breasts. My lover is to me a cluster of henna blossoms" (Song of Songs 1:13–14). The softness of his hair perhaps reminds her of the softness of the flower's blossoms. Our marriages would be immeasurably enriched if we could learn from this couple how to affirm one another.

When did you last affirm or praise your mate for personal qualities or attributes (patience, kindness, a good attitude through a difficult situation, thoroughness, thoughtfulness, etc.)? Do you often thank him/her for simple gestures of practical helpfulness? Have you learned how to praise your spouse in terms of hairstyle, dress, jewelry, or fragrance? Do you avoid put-downs and cutting remarks, both in the privacy of your home, and especially in the presence of others? Your words of affirmation, praise, and appreciation, if genuinely expressed as the way you see your mate, can generate sparks of romance and passion. Our words have an amazing power to affect our actions, even altering our attitude and disposition.

Marital Love With Passion And Adventure

This couple also knew how to keep their love story alive. In just four verses of chapter seven, there is a wonderful, romantic adventure *initiated by the wife!* I do not mean to shock the reader. Some may feel that even *marital* lovemaking should be held privately in one's heart as a personal and intimate secret. I simply feel that it is important we understand God's Word, and be open enough to be instructed by it.

This love episode begins with the woman's stated confidence in her sexuality. "I belong to my lover, and his desire is for me" (Song of Songs 7:10). She proposes that they explore the countryside and do an overnight in one of the villages. "Come, my lover, let us go to the countryside, let us spend the night in the villages" (7:11). They of course tell their friends that they are going to see if their family vineyards are yet budding, and whether the pomegranates are yet in bloom. Privately she confides her underlying motivation with her husband. "There I will give you my love" (7:12). There is something more happening here than an overnight visit to a friend's home in one of the neighboring villages, because she emphasizes her desire to offer her love to him.

Then, as if that were not enough to stir him into action, she reminds him that "every delicacy" is at their door (7:13). We are left to decide whether she is referring to exotic foods, or to their favorite experiences of making love. If she is merely referring to food, she has shifted her focus, because she was talking about giving her love to him. These "delicacies" are then more fully elaborated as "both new and old, that I have stored up for you, my lover." Does not she mean much more than enjoying a special dinner comprising new recipes and old favorites? She plans to give him her love! I do not want to be dogmatic about this interpretation, but while my mind says it could be either, my heart says that she is still on the subject of love. I also have the feeling that the horses were in readiness at the front door in record time! And the clear inference is that before the day ended, they had made love in the privacy of their vineyard: "Let us go early to the vineyards . . . there I will give you my love" (7:12).

This wife apparently does not have a lot of sexual inhibitions and hang-ups for we discover several verses later that one of their lasting memories as husband and wife was when she "roused" him "under the apple tree," her love for him burning like a "blazing fire, like a mighty flame" (Song of Songs 8:5–6). How else can we interpret this scripture? Surely he had not simply been "roused" from sleep, for she goes on to speak of her love as being like a "blazing fire" and "a mighty flame" (8:6). What husband would not like this kind of overnight date with his wife? What wife would not enjoy being this confident and alive in her flirtations with her husband? I find myself wishing that Joanne and I owned a vineyard somewhere in the secluded countryside!

There is another saga of romance in *The Song of Songs*, which begins with the wife waking up during the early morning hours to discover that she cannot snuggle up to her husband—he is gone! She looks for him throughout the house, but she cannot find him. "I looked for the one my heart loves; I looked for him but did not find him" (Song of Songs 3:1). Had he remembered an important early morning business appointment somewhere in the city? Was he a forgetful guy? Was she always reminding him? Did she know the places he often met for business matters? She quickly gets dressed and heads into town to find him. "I will search for the one my heart loves" (3:2).

When her first few guesses are not fruitful, she asks one of the city watchmen making his rounds, "Have you seen the one my heart loves?" (3:3b). This gal is not shy. And do you get the feeling this was not the first time this watchman had helped her find her man? The guard surely went home to tell his story about finding Mrs. Smith romantically stalking her husband again, wanting to have a rendezvous with him. There is nothing wrong with having an affair at the office, so long as the man is your husband (or the woman is your wife)! This time the watchman was not knowledgeable about her husband's whereabouts, but no sooner had she said goodbye to him than she finds "the one my heart loves" (3:4b).

Then we come upon this remarkable statement about what happens next. "I held him and would not let him go till I had brought him to my mother's house, to the room of the one who conceived me" (3:4). *That had to be Mom's bedroom!* We can only guess that Mom lived right there in the heart of the business district, and the daughter knew that Mom would only encourage their passionate love by providing them with the privacy of her bedroom. Mom had very likely not forgotten her own flirtatious adventures with her own husband. I cannot believe they were there to borrow a dozen eggs!

Her mom may have been recently widowed, as there is no mention of her husband. If so, was her bedroom still decorated with a romantic touch? Did her mother still have many beautiful memories of her husband and his love for her? Wasn't this the very best meeting place that the daughter could think of to complete her determined date with her husband? Reading between the lines, I also have the impression that this husband was not kicking and yelling in protest, as his wife kept her arms wrapped around his waist, taking her beloved down to Mom's, perhaps just a block or so away. "When I found the one my heart loves I held him and would not let him go till I had brought him to my mother's house" (Song of Songs 3:4). Are we to assume that she was not about to wait until they took the long ride back to their suburban home? What a lovely glimpse into the joy and adventure of a lively marriage!

Do we have that kind of wholesome sexual freedom, joyousness, family support, and openness in our marriages within our own culture? If we do, I have not seen much evidence of it from my particular vantage point. Who would not welcome such a wholesome freedom, joy, and spontaneity within the circle of their family? Who would not love to have a mother-in-law who would gladly give her full support to her daughter's desires to be with her husband intimately?

If they found Mom home (and not at the market shopping), let me assure you that this highly committed couple in this warm familial context did not first sit down calmly to visit Mom for fifteen or twenty minutes! Instead, I would guess that this wonderful mom went to her kitchen smiling to prepare refreshments for the three of them to enjoy later. As she put together some refreshments or lunch, did she recall with delight her own wonderful experiences with her husband? When the three of them then sat together, was Mom given a sketchy summary of the couple's frustrating morning, but ultimately memorable day? I can hear the husband saying, "Mom, you have a very strong-willed, heartless daughter! My side still hurts from her wrenching hug. She held me as tightly as a stadium wrestler for the entire two blocks! I could not have escaped if I wanted to!"

This scriptural story about a married couple's romantic rendez-vous with one another may be some three thousand years old, but it has so much spontaneity, creativity, wholesomeness, color, and integrity that it remains for me a standard bearer for a vital joyous marriage and a passionate love that burns like a "blazing fire" (Song of Songs 8:6). True intimacy and joy occur within the committed and faithful relationship of Christian marriage, and not in an uncommitted or under-committed relationship that has no real security or constancy, and no strong vows of two wills to undergird the bond of love throughout their entire future—come what may.

In summary, truths to be learned from Song of Songs are these:

1. Your sexuality is a special and remarkable gift of God, built into your physical and spiritual makeup so as to enable you, within the covenant of marriage, to provide your partner (and reciprocally, yourself) with experiences of exquisite joy and delight.

2. Because God is the designer of this remarkable capacity, we need to speak about the sexual experience and our bodies generally with respect, avoiding any words or expressions that dishonor this wondrous, joy-giving experience between a husband and a wife, especially as we instruct our children in the meaning of their own sexuality approaching puberty and beyond. We have absolutely no reason for regarding any part of our bodies with shame or disgust, and there is no aspect of the act of marital foreplay or intercourse that is obscene or "dirty."

3. We need to learn how to affirm one another verbally, helping our mate know what particularly pleases us in terms

of personal attributes, loving gestures, practical helpfulness, a sensitive understanding, jewelry, dress, etc.

4. Both husband and wife need to learn how to creatively relate to one another in celebrative experiences of adventure and romance that become treasured memories and serve to deepen their love story and keep it renewed and spontaneous, fresh and exciting.

The Challenge of Interpreting Scripture Correctly

The Song of Songs, at least for me, is one of the more challenging books of the Bible to interpret or understand. Generally speaking, the older the writing, the more difficult it is to understand. *The Song of Songs* is about three thousand years old—one of the oldest books of the Bible. It is probably also true, generally speaking, that the older the writing the more diverse the interpretations. For example, some scholars have concluded that we have just one seamless love song here, while others feel that it was originally a collection of individual love songs carefully seamed together to give it a measure of congruity and flow.

I personally believe that *The Song of Songs* is a collection of love songs that were originally viewed as beautiful expressions of marital love—songs that were useful in helping the ancient community of Israel to understand the purpose of marriage as God intended it to be. It depicts the exquisite joy God wanted to give us through the marriage bond with its beautiful sexual expressions. It may be that the title *The Song of Songs* was not intended to mean that this is the *ultimate* or *best* love song. Rather, it may mean that this "song of songs" is *a compilation of songs*, a uniquely long love song that was created by collecting and carefully fusing together several widely appreciated love ballads or poems that had some common features, as well as some unique content. Over time they were brilliantly strung together, perhaps for the purpose of publicly presenting and joyously celebrating the vitality and freedom of marriage as God intended it to be for us. The repeated "refrains" that say something like, "How beautiful you are and how pleasing!" might be a part of the structuring of the song that makes the transitions smooth and gives it a certain singleness and flow.

Whatever you conclude, I would encourage you to take the time to thoughtfully read this remarkable love song and decide for yourself. However you interpret this treasure in God's Word, I believe that you will be amazed by its insight and beauty and its capacity to offer all marriages a greater wisdom, insight, and depth of joy.

However we interpret and understand *The Song of Songs,* one thing that seems to be altogether clear is that the bride, and reciprocally the groom, are virgins on their wedding night—a value that has been largely lost in our culture today. It is not simply a matter of following certain patterns of etiquette, societal regulations, or accepted social customs. Virginity until marriage is a part of God's plan to insure that our marriage will be one that lasts. God intends that the fullness of sexuality as an expression of love needs to occur simultaneously with the greatest strength of relationship that we can possibly achieve. That's why our "vows" of commitment before the community of faith are so vitally important.

Those public vows hold us accountable for a lifetime, and therefore provide our marriage with such strength of relationship and such a permanence in terms of our love for one another that we will remain together "in sickness and in health, until death do us part." Our children should not have to fear the breakup of the home, but rather have before them daily living role models that are totally committed to a lifetime of fidelity, both "in joy and in sorrow" as long as both partners live.

Whether *The Song of Songs* is to be understood as a chronological description of the courtship of two lovers, their wedding day, and their years of marriage, or simply a cherished collection of sensitive love themes and stories about any God-honoring marriage, we can be sure that maintaining our virginity prior to marriage is a primary and crucial characteristic of this biblical writing. Here is a helpful and inspiring portrait of a marriage that overflows with love and joy because of the couple's faithfulness to God's will for their union, and their understanding that this is for keeps.

Integrating

The Song of Songs is one of the shorter books of the Bible, with just eight chapters. In my *New International Version* it is just shy of ten pages long. The partners in this portrayed marriage describe (using many colorful metaphors) the mate's attractiveness and beauty, and what aspects of his or her body give them an adrenaline rush. If you were to write down your own romantic adventures with your wife/ husband, and what excites you when you are alone together, would you end up with ten pages to tell your own love story? Or would you need only five? *Or just two!* I suspect that most of us would have to stretch ourselves to come up with ten pages of romantic dialogue and daring excursions having the color, joy, intimacy, creativity, adventure, boldness, freedom, and openness of this couple in *The Song of Songs.* Why is this so? And can we change the way we think about sex and the way we make love with our partner?

Ending the Silence on Sexuality in Our Homes

What you are about to read is the most important page in this book. I have nothing to say elsewhere in this book that is as significant a concern as the concern discussed here. It has to do with our role as Christian parents to talk with our children about God's gift of sexuality and our responsibility to God in terms of our use of it. Millions of parents in America are absolutely silent about the whole topic of sexuality for any number of reasons—lack of confidence, fear of saying the wrong thing, trusting our schools to give all the information needed, the conviction that our teens will not respect what we say anyway, procrastination, our lack of time due to our pressured schedules, and conflicting opinions between Mom and Dad as to how to approach this sensitive issue—to cite just a few. I only need to remind you that our public schools are charged with instructing our children and youth about how our sexual organs work and how pregnancy and childbirth occur, *but they do not have the authority or freedom to "impose" values, or to include God's purpose or biblical teachings on this subject.* This critical part of preparing our children with respect to their sexuality falls back on the parents and the home—as it should.

If we fail to talk intelligently with our children about the wonder of their sexuality, we will put them in an extremely vulnerable and even dangerous position. *And they will undoubtedly run into opinions about sex elsewhere.* Various perspectives will come to them from their well-intentioned peers, from glitzy magazines, a stumbled-upon web site, or a graffiti-filled restroom wall—whatever their experiences, they will surely be exposed to the perspectives of others. And you can be sure that 90 percent of it will not even come close to what God wants us to understand about the appropriate, God-ordained expression of our sexuality. God's purpose is undoubtedly targeting a lifetime of fulfillment and happiness within the security and strength of the marriage bond. Because his goal is infinitely higher, it will require more thoughtful preparation, self-discipline, and abstinence—none of which are required if the only goal is to have "fun," regardless of the cost.

To reiterate, the home that is silent about this most important and most personal issue places the child or youth in an extremely vulnerable and dangerous position. When the day comes that a member of the opposite sex tries to "love" talk your youth into sexual intimacy without any parental instruction or dialogue about personal security, commitment, or the permanence that marriage vows promise, your child or youth may not be able to say "no" to the promiscuous advances and the incredibly good physical feelings that come with touch. Who among the young could possibly anticipate how incredibly wonderful it feels? And if pregnancy occurs, and the man (more likely, boy) walks away from the woman (more likely, girl), her life is absolutely transformed. She now has the role of mother—a role that becomes a major focus for her life. *The parental role is not a twenty-year-long responsibility. You are a parent through your entire lifetime!*

What God intended to be one of the supreme acts of joy in our lives, experienced in the secure and permanent commitment of marriage, instead becomes a "burden" that catches us at a moment when we are extremely uninformed and unprepared. The daunting options offered for unwanted pregnancies, unwanted fetuses, and unwanted babies is most often abortion—a choice which seems to be a quick resolution on the surface, but has a very high, long-term emotional price tag for a young woman. (The risk in a premature or spontaneous sexual act is additionally compounded if the inviter or enticer has a contagious, sexually-transmitted disease.)

Do you see why it is absolutely essential that we sit down with our kids and talk candidly about God's high purposes for their lives, which include the wonder of sexual experience within the security and strength of Christian marriage? That is to say, a committed marriage needs to be obedient to the life of Christ, joyously including vows of love that anticipate a lifetime together, whether "in sickness or in health, as long as we both shall live." *Even with the most basic understanding of what God wants for us in terms of our sexuality, who would carelessly or casually waste such a great treasure entrusted to us by God for our own lasting joy?*

If your grandfather left your nine-year-old child a collection of family jewelry having a value of about a million dollars, would you simply give them to your child to play with as he will? Of course not! You would try to help your child understand what a tremendous gift his grand-pop had given him. You would also take immediate measures to protect the gift until the child had matured enough to understand how to use the gift wisely and appropriately. So, too, with his sexuality. Sexuality is a priceless gift given to us by our Creator, and if we can help our child understand just how precious it is, his life will be enriched by it and not crippled by its misuse. Without that help from the parent, the provision of the grandparent would be carelessly lost or soon squandered away.

I urge you to make a personal commitment to Christ as a parent and make it your family creed to talk with your children about the joy God wants them to experience again and again as a result of being created as spiritual and sexual beings. Tell them why such an incredible gift from God deserves the protection which only restraint, self-discipline, abstinence, and a growing understanding of God's will can serve to protect it. This is also why the longer term "courtship" is a more appropriate path to a satisfying, lifelong marriage relationship.

Only as we enter into marriage do we make a public commitment to remain united—come what may! Our marriage vows are an act of the will and not the fleeting feeling of the moment, which could change from one day to the next.

Therein lies our potential for the greatest and most lasting joys. Whereas many other paths may "feel right" at the moment, they will ultimately be seen as a poor choice—cheating us of the permanence and happiness of a lifetime commitment to one another, regardless of what we face together.

(For those planning to make a personal commitment to God to begin a conversation with their children about their God-given sexuality, please turn to the prayer at the end of the chapter.)

How Would You Handle This Situation?

How did you learn about sex? Many of us did not learn about sex in our home because it was not talked about. And how are *you* processing the topic of sexuality with *your* children and adolescents? Is your home any different from the one in which you were raised? Let us suppose that six-year-old Ben comes to Mom with this question. "Mom, I came out of your tummy—right?" (We are assuming that Ben is already familiar with the word "penis" as a result of earlier intentional family instruction. He knows that word as a part of his body, not unlike his knowledge of his "shoulders" or "eyebrows." Knowing all this, Mom feels as if she has more options than the parent who has to stop and introduce a new term, or interrupt her own focus to deal with a word's definition. She is free to use such terms if needed, or to answer his question some other way.)

"That's exactly right, Ben," says Mom, while putting the groceries away. (Why do children always ask their more significant questions while you're putting away ten bags of mostly perishable items?)

"But how did I get there—I mean, inside you? Did God put me there?"

"Ben, that's a very good question. A question that Mommy would love to try to answer. Let us do this—go hang up your coat and put your backpack up in your room, and I will finish putting the groceries away. And then we will sit down and talk. Would you like a hot chocolate?"

"Yeah!" Excitedly, Ben runs out of the room, does the two simple chores enthusiastically, and is back in the kitchen before the hot chocolate is ready!

"I have not forgotten your question," says Mom. "But first, how did you do on your ecology project for Mr. Clearwater?" Ben is still chatting when the microwave beeps, and Mom puts the two hot chocolates on the table along with a half-empty bag of marshmallows.

Then Mom starts off. "Ben, your question was, how did you get into my tummy, right? And you thought that God had something to do with it? Is that what you're asking?"

"Uh-huh," says Ben, glancing up quickly between stirring his hot chocolate and watching the marshmallows busily circling in his cup.

"Well, God did have a lot to do with you being in my tummy, but God made Mommy and Daddy in a special way that Daddy and I have a lot to do with it too!" Mom looks at Ben to see if he's listening. He's really into his hot chocolate, but he's also looking up at her between sips. So she continues.

"When Mommy and Daddy get you tucked into bed at the end of the day and kiss you goodnight, we soon head to bed ourselves. And before we go to sleep, we often want to show each other how much we love one another with a few kisses and hugs. But when you're a Mommy and Daddy, you simply enjoy being in each other's arms for a while."

Ben interrupts with a somewhat scrunched face, "But doesn't that get boring after awhile?"

"Not at all! In fact, it feels very special for both the Mommy and Daddy. And I hope that someday, you will marry someone you love as much as Daddy loves me, and can share that wonderful feeling together."

While Mom is thinking about where to go next with this, she notices Ben's interest is fading, and so she quickly winds it up with, "And when the Daddy and Mommy get together like that and feel so happy with one another, there could be the tiniest beginning of a special baby to be named Ben!"

But Ben, who probably understood only about a quarter of the entire conversation, has already disconnected. "Mom, can I have some more marshmallows in my hot chocolate?" Ben lost all interest once he found out that the Mommy and Daddy have to persevere through the boredom of a long series of hugs and kisses if a baby is to be the outcome! And so, suddenly we come to the abrupt end of our educational session! But Mom made a very good effort, giving her inquisitive son enough explanation and information to satisfy him—probably for months. His Mom also has a better understanding about Ben's view of cuddling and kissing!

This kind of family conversation is challenging. Afterward, you may realize upon reflection or after sharing it with your spouse, that you were trying to give more information than your child required. Or you may conclude that you were playing it too safe—giving instruction or offering explanations that were too vague to be very helpful. However you grade this particular mom, she did exceptionally well in setting up the conversation so that Ben was focused, and she would not be distracted by her own chores. Such questions by the child deserve our fullest attention. She was also able to monitor how well Ben was listening throughout the conversation, and noticed when his questions had been sufficiently satisfied. There was also another big plus. The effort gave Mom some useful experience and a greater confidence when she and Ben have their next conversation about sexuality.

The next conversation will wait for another day—possibly while Mom is in the middle of an appointment with an interior designer discussing the renovation of her kitchen, or frantically getting the house ready for a dinner gathering with several close friends. And, if she's really lucky, Ben may ask Dad!

I encourage you to be courageous, yet humble, in responding to your child's searching questions. Trust God to give you the sensitive words that will help your child gradually discover the God-given purpose for his/her own emerging sexuality. Then he/she will begin to understand how priceless it is as a gift of God—and therefore guard it.

Some Practical Suggestions

- Arguments and anger that occur during the day, either in the home or over the phone, carry over into the night. You cannot possibly expect your mate to respond warmly or enthusiastically to your advances if you have been accusing, bitter, or sarcastic with her/him during the day. "Therefore, as God's chosen people, holy and dearly loved, clothe yourselves with compassion, kindness, humility, gentleness and patience. Bear with each other and forgive whatever grievances you may have against one another" (Col. 3:12–13).

- Lovemaking is always more passionate if each partner does his/her fair share of the parenting and housekeeping needs, such as playing softball with your son in the back yard, helping with your daughter's science project, doing the dishes after supper, or overseeing teeth-brushing and tucking the kids into bed. If you each share in the responsibilities of maintaining a healthy family life and a stable, orderly home, you will more likely want to snuggle up to your thoughtful "helpmate." When the responsibilities of family are shared fairly, neither of you will be exhausted at the end of the day! "Carry each other's burdens, and in this way you will fulfill the law of Christ" (Gal. 6:2).

- Be aware of the fact that activities for your kids that are too heavily scheduled, too much overtime at the workplace, too large a house to clean and maintain, or some combination of these factors, will probably mean that you are very often feeling overwhelmed and exhausted by the end of the day and will not want to make love. Lovemaking requires some energy output and also a relaxed body and mind. Reducing the sports and activities of your kids, allowing activities for yourselves as a couple (such as ballroom dancing, a concert series, shopping for antiques, etc.), downsizing your house, or simplifying your landscaping may all help to bring you to the close of the day less frazzled.

- We are not in need of more books that offer new or exotic positions for sex. What we need to learn in lovemaking is how to more graciously give of ourselves, how to find joy in simply giving fully from the heart. A spouse who begins lovemaking with a personal intention and desire to give fully to the other will find that there are both immediate satisfactions (like hearing your lover's sighs) and future rewards (like learning together how to be better lovers). And when *both* husband and wife act selflessly in the way they offer themselves to one another, you have ultimate sex! Even in making love, "It is more blessed to give than to receive" (Acts 20:35).

- I enjoy occasionally planning a six-hour "date" with Joanne—especially when we are on vacation—often with the events of the entire evening being a surprise for her. She knows when our evening will begin, but the events of the evening are usually a surprise. An evening may include: a romantic dinner at her favorite restaurant, a movie or play she will enjoy, a walk in the park or on the beach, biking at sunset, an hour or so at her favorite mall or bookstore, dessert at an ice-cream parlor, a relaxing bubble bath set up with candlelight, and so on. Be sure your mate knows beforehand what she/he will need for the evening—walking shoes, a sweater, slacks (rather than a skirt), sunglasses, etc. Conclude your evening at an hour when you're not totally exhausted if you are planning to enjoy some time with each other. (Note: Some do not care for "surprises." If your spouse is such a person, give her/him a preview of your plans for the evening. In such cases, your spouse will still enjoy your advance preparations for an enjoyable well-planned "date"!)

A Prayer

Lord of all creation, who entertained a great risk to freely give us an indescribable joy through our sexuality within marriage, help me as a parent to risk talking to our children about this all-important topic. I confess that I have remained silent for too many years because I felt fearful that I might say the wrong thing. It always felt more comfortable to postpone it rather than to plan as husband and wife how to do it wisely and with your Spirit present with us to guide our words and thoughts. Teach us as parents how to do this humbly, thoughtfully, and sensitively, so that our child (children) may adopt a strategy that protects this priceless gift of yours through their own personal commitment to self-discipline, restraint, abstinence, and especially to understand in a fuller way your will for their lives. Thank you for the wonder of love and sexuality that you have entrusted to us, and teach us to be wise, both as parents and as a child, using your gift exactly as you intended. In Jesus' name I pray. Amen.

Three Questions

1. Do you agree that our children are "endangered" and made "vulnerable" as a result of our being silent as parent(s) about the meaning of their sexuality and what God's intentions are for its appropriate use? Why are these two words appropriate to use?

2. If you are studying this book with others, you may want to consider making a covenant with each other that you will talk with your child/children about sexuality and support one another in the process. If so, you will want to specifically determine whether everyone is willing to receive helpful and sensitive feedback from the group concerning any efforts you make about such conversations and whether you will pray for one another about this important ongoing process.

3. How would you evaluate Ben's mother, as one who is trying to enter into a conversation with her young son about the meaning of his God-given sexuality? How well did she do? Be as specific as you can.

INSIGHTS

Success in marriage consists not only in finding the right mate, but also in being the right mate.

—Anonymous

An archeologist is the best husband a woman can have; the older she gets, the more interested he is in her.

—Agatha Christie

Sexual information without relation to values is intellectually irresponsible.

—Peter A. Bertocci

Marriage is not just spiritual communion and passionate embraces; marriage is also three-meals-a-day and remembering to carry out the trash.

—Joyce Brothers

There is a tendency to think of sex as something degrading; it is not; it is magnificent, an enormous privilege, but because of that the rules are tremendously strict and severe.

—Francis Devas

Modern man refuses to recognize that God has set certain standards, certain absolutes for sex, as he has for behavior generally. To be ignorant of these absolutes, or to deny them or rationalize them, in no way invalidates them.

—L. Nelson Bell

Continence (meaning total abstinence from sexual activity) is the only guarantee of an undefiled spirit, and the best protection against the promiscuity that cheapens and finally kills the power to love.

—Gene Tunney (in an address to youth)

We pray that the young men and women of today and tomorrow will grow up with the realization that sex is a beautiful flame they carry in the lantern of their bodies.

—Demetrius Monousos

When Jesus reached the spot, he looked up and said to him, "Zacchaeus, come down immediately. I must stay at your house today." So he came down at once and welcomed him gladly. All the people saw this and began to mutter, "He has gone to be the guest of a 'sinner.'"

—Luke 19:5–7

The Utmost Respect

INTERPERSONAL

As a young married man, I was surprised by how much time my wife spent on the phone keeping in touch with her girlfriends. It never became an issue between us, but I must say that in my inner thoughts I held this notion that women are a bit gossipy and could be more useful if they did not waste so much time chatting on the telephone. Joanne had many other wonderful qualities as a young woman, so her excessive phone time remained small stuff for me.

I see it all very differently now. Today Joanne sits comfortably on our sofa while talking with her girlfriends, spending even more time today than she did in her twenties. Through the years, life has dealt some heavy blows to her girlfriends. One calls Joanne because her husband is losing his battle with cancer. Another friend, a widow, is dealing with cancer herself and is largely without support and encouragement. Another is increasingly in touch with her because her grandchildren are using drugs and getting into trouble.

Joanne is giving these persons encouragement, love, gentle and wise counsel, and her total support and full attention. She never loads the dishwasher or folds the laundry while she talks. She often shares some light stories about our granddaughters or tells other anecdotes that will help her friends forget their troubles for a moment and laugh. She patiently listens for as long as it takes her troubled friends to unburden themselves.

Joanne's supportive phone conversations are a special ministry that only a few can do as lovingly as she does it. My respect for Joanne has grown through the years as I have come to understand why she spends so much of her time encouraging and cheering up her girlfriends. This personal ministry requires hundreds of intense and focused hours each year.

Joanne and I at times retire early after a busy day. Occasionally she will get an unexpected late call from one of her close friends. During the first minute or so of the call, Joanne will find a comfortable position on our sofa, a position that allows her to totally focus on her friend's concerns or pain. The call will undoubtedly last at least half an hour. Rather than complaining or whimpering, I respect her time on the phone and marvel at her capacity to be so concerned and compassionate, especially when she has had a long, tiring day herself. She loves not only me deeply, but also our dear friends who possibly need her love and understanding at that moment more than I do. Because I fully respect what she is doing, I will gladly share her with others.

INSPIRING

> Jesus entered Jericho and was passing through. A man was there by the name of Zacchaeus; he was a chief tax collector and was wealthy. He wanted to see who Jesus was, but being a short man he could not, because of the crowd. So he ran ahead and climbed a sycamore-fig tree to see him, since Jesus was coming that way. When Jesus reached the spot, he looked up and said to him, "Zacchaeus, come down immediately. I must stay at your house today." So he came down at once and welcomed him gladly. All the people saw this and began to mutter, "He has gone to be the guest of a sinner." But Zacchaeus stood up and said to the Lord, "Look, Lord! Here and now I give half of my possessions to the poor, and if I have cheated anybody out of anything, I will pay back four times the amount." Jesus said to him, "Today salvation has come to this house, because this man, too, is a son of Abraham. For the Son of Man came to seek and to save what was lost."
>
> —Luke 19:1–10

Imagining

A Letter from Zacchaeus to His Nephew

Zacchaeus sends greetings to my esteemed nephew, Gaius, Rome's most distinguished centurion in Syria, with fond memories of our last visit in glorious Damascus. It was a pleasure for me to be included in the dedication of the new barracks and stables and to see your well-trained horsemen perform. Your disciplined command these past several years is no doubt the major reason for these successes.

I wanted to let you know that you probably have a better uncle now, as a result of a surprising visitor to our city. I am referring to the very one who healed your servant several weeks ago, the man called Jesus, the Christ. Your son, of course, told me the story in detail about how Jesus healed Abar despite the fact that he was over a mile from your house. I have to confess that I took it as a coincidence that your servant boy got well that same day. Young Anthony was so excited about how it all happened that I did not want to dampen his spirit. I must admit that I enjoyed hearing his great enthusiasm for Jesus. Now that I have had my own opportunity to meet Jesus, I wish to apologize to both you and Anthony for taking the matter so casually. Whoever this man is, he should not be taken lightly. Every time I think about meeting Jesus, I have to smile about the entire day. Let me tell you what happened.

There were so many rumors flying around Jericho concerning this man. One man told me that he saw ten lepers healed by Jesus in the time it takes to get a horse into a full run! The woman who does my marketing told me without blushing that he rescued several of his friends who very nearly perished in a violent storm at sea. And get this! He saved them by calmly talking it over with the storm! Well, needless to say, such stories are preposterous rumors, but they still intrigued me enough that I wanted to have a look at this man myself. When I learned he was coming through Jericho, I thought I might get to see one or two of his remarkable deceptions.

Our main street was thick with people the day he arrived. I knew I was in trouble. I think I told you how all three pairs of my recently acquired stirrups had to be re-cut because I am so short. I figured that all I would see would be a wall of shoulders and backs. As you know, I am not much on etiquette, so I climbed one of those twisted sycamore trees. I got a few glaring looks, but I am used to that kind of thing. Besides, the foliage protected me from their stares. At any rate, I had a fine view of the entire street.

It never occurred to me that this new celebrity would stop at my tree! I felt kind of foolish, perched up in the tree and dressed as I was with gold rings on every finger! When Jesus looked up and called me by name, as if I was an old friend of his, it did something to me. Instead of poking fun at me for my bizarre behavior, he gave me his respect and interest. He looked right into my eyes, warmth in his easy smile, as he said, "Zacchaeus, come down here!" He sounded like you—comfortable giving orders. Then came the biggest surprise of all! Decisively, he said, "I *have* to stay at your house today!" He made it sound as if I was one of his important appointments! So I came scampering down like a schoolboy. I felt as though a massive door had opened before me. It seemed as if I was passing through a huge gateway and being welcomed into a new life. No one had ever taken me that seriously or welcomed my friendship as warmly as Jesus did that day.

In the few moments it took to get out of the tree, something happened inside me. It was as though all of life's possibilities were standing before me. I could see persons in the crowd who looked aghast that Jesus would be *my* guest at *his* invitation! But even their muttering did not bother me. Jesus gave me a vision of life's possibilities. All those folks could be my friends. We could change our mutual hostility into neighborliness.

You will not believe this but your uncle Zaccheaus, who has been recognized by Rome for his capacity to collect enormous taxes, said right there on the spot, "Look, Lord! Here and now I pledge half of all I own to the poor." And if that was not enough to bewilder the crowd, I went on almost recklessly, "If I have cheated *anyone* out of *anything*, I will pay back four times the amount!" When I glanced up at Jesus, he was smiling with approval and encouragement. I will never forget what he said: "This very day salvation has come to this man's house, because he too is a son of Abraham." I felt that this man

Jesus was lining me up with all those who had walked in the footsteps of Abraham, the Jews' greatest man of faith. Can you imagine me standing in *that* line-up! I felt so trusted and respected.

When Jesus left that evening, I was undoubtedly the happiest man in Jericho. I thought I would regret all that I had promised. I feared that this hope-filled feeling would be gone in a day or so. But it has now been more than a week, and I am still feeling high! I have already paid back some of my neighbors whom I cheated years ago, and some are actually coming to my door with their grievances, feeling convinced—perhaps by a neighbor—that I meant what I said! It has been a joy to see their initial uneasiness when stepping into my imposing house and then seeing them leave with a bag of money. I felt I was a man who was now genuinely honest for the first time in his life—a man who could potentially be a neighbor and friend, a man they could trust and respect. What an irony! To think that Jesus would treat me with dignity and respect, surely the very last thing I deserved!

When all my debts are settled, I will probably have only a fraction of my former wealth. But I still consider myself to be one of the richest men in Jericho. I am investing heavily in a whole new line-up that I never considered before—things like love, peace, kindness, and generosity!

Let me know when we can spend a few days together. You will undoubtedly want to meet your altogether altered and upgraded uncle as soon as possible! Please share this letter with Anthony and your entire family, including Abar. May the peace that Jesus brings fill your heart. May his grace and love be with you and your entire household!

INTERPRETING

The word *respect* occurs in the Bible only two or three dozen times, depending on the translation being considered. However, the Scriptures additionally provide many excellent illustrations of respect in the lives of people. Respect has to do with holding a person in esteem and with treating that person with consideration and courtesy. As an illustration, consider the two blind men mentioned in

Matthew 20:29–34. The two men heard that Jesus was passing by, along with a huge crowd. Because these men were blind, they could not be sure just how close Jesus was to them, so they shouted loudly for Jesus. The crowd found their yelling offensive and disrespectful, especially since it was directed toward Jesus. In fact, a few in the crowd just as disrespectfully told the two men to shut up. But these blind men must have heard enough about Jesus' miracles and healings to know that this moment could be their only chance in a lifetime to be healed. So they simply yelled louder! Jesus graciously overlooks their unrefined conduct and becomes a servant to them. He asks them, "What do you want me to do for you?" (Matt. 20:32).

The two men state their need clearly and concisely: "Lord, we want our sight" (Matt. 2:33). And Jesus, without hesitation, responds to their request with compassion and respect. He treats them no differently than he would have treated a nobleman, a governor, or a centurion. They are at once able to see. This first biblical passage suggests through Jesus' example that we are to regard a surprisingly wide circle of persons with respect. If we are to treat the blind beggar on the street or the homeless person respectfully, surely our spouse is included among those we are to hold daily in esteem and treat with the utmost consideration and courtesy.

But My Spouse Does Not Deserve Respect!

You may be thinking along these lines: "Those blind men had an extremely difficult life. So we can rejoice that Jesus compassionately set them free from their desperate situation. If that had been me, I too would have shouted for Jesus at the top of my lungs! Besides, there is nothing in the biblical passage that suggests that the men had done anything terribly wrong. Unlike the blind men, my spouse is self-centered. He thinks only of himself. He is unreasonably tight with our money, he never does his fair share of caring for the children, and he has no interest in maintaining our home. So he first needs to earn my respect!"

If some of those feelings resonate with you, you will be interested in knowing what Scripture offers by way of a quite different position. Let us examine another biblical model for respect that again involves

Jesus. The person he is relating to is Zacchaeus, a tax gatherer residing in a handsome mansion in suburban Jericho. Zacchaeus most likely gained his wealth by collecting several kinds of taxes under Roman authority. The people of Jericho would have seen him as a traitor to the nation of Israel. The Roman system of taxation in subject nations like Israel encouraged corruption. To state it simply, Rome decided how much tax money a given city should contribute to the Roman Empire, and the tax agent was responsible for delivering that amount annually to the appropriate Roman authorities. However, the tax agent was also free to tax beyond that amount to secure his own earnings or salary. This arrangement led to corruption, greed, and excess. At times, it led to taxes so exorbitant that the tax collector became extremely wealthy and, at the same time, a much-hated public figure. Such a person was Zacchaeus.

Zacchaeus was a small man who, in all likelihood, lived in an imposing house. When he learned that Jesus was to visit Jericho, he wanted to meet him. Perhaps Zacchaeus was simply curious. Perhaps he had heard of Jesus' miracles. Possibly he was drawn to Jesus because of his much cited and much discussed teachings. He may have wanted to see one of Jesus' miracles and to decide for himself whether it was a hoax or the work of an authentic power. Whatever drew him to Jesus, this little man of great wealth found himself in a sycamore tree, probably in ostentatious dress and jewelry, waiting to see Jesus pass by. He was comfortable doing this not because he was eccentric, but more likely because he was a man who met his goals. He would have had no reason in the world to suppose that *anyone* would come to talk with him that day, *especially Jesus!*

With all that in mind, you can be certain that anyone in charge of Jesus' itinerary would have carefully avoided Zacchaeus. The man was a cheat. He was hated by everyone who knew him. His name suggests that he was an Israelite, but he was a traitor to Israel. The thinking of the people of Jericho went something like this: If Jesus really is concerned about the poor, if he really is the Holy One of Israel, the awaited Messiah, he will have absolutely nothing to do with that scoundrel Zacchaeus!

Now consider what Jesus does. Not a single word on his lips belittles or scorns this man. He offers not a single hint of criticism or judgment. Jesus accuses him of nothing. He does not even require this man to confess his thieving ways or make a public apology. Jesus not only knows his name, but he also protects him from embarrassment. Jesus goes so far as to invite himself to Zacchaeus's home, knowing that Zacchaeus would never think of being the host for Jesus. Zacchaeus knew nothing about extending an invitation or offering hospitality anyway. Contrastingly, Jesus runs the risk of being seen as a total disappointment and disgrace to the entire population of Jericho, simply by extending his hand and friendship to this miserable piece of humanity. Was there ever anyone so utterly respected that was so unworthy, so undeserving, so unqualified?

This episode between Jesus and Zacchaeus raises the bar of respect considerably. If the likes of a Zacchaeus is to be given respect from all of us who bear the name of Christ, then doesn't this mean that even the husband who swears too much or the wife who habitually overloads the credit cards must also be treated respectfully? If that is not what this biblical account is teaching, what is it saying? Why does Jesus take such an approach? What is he hoping to achieve? Probably something similar to Zacchaeus's transformation. He comes out of the tree a changed man, determined to live his life differently, more honestly, more generously, more graciously, and one can say as well, more Christlike.

The Urge to Kill!

One of the most intriguing and thought-provoking accounts in the Bible is the story of two brothers, one of whom was so deceitfully treated by his own brother that he made a vow to kill his brother once their ailing father Isaac passed away. It was Esau who vowed: "He [Jacob] has deceived me these two times: He took my birthright, and now he's taken my blessing! . . . The days of mourning for my father are near; *then I will kill my brother Jacob*" (Gen. 27:36, 41, emphasis mine).

What had Jacob done that had so incensed his brother, Esau? How could a stolen "birthright" or a stolen "blessing" cause a brother to cool-headedly prepare to murder his twin? In the first place, the birthright was stolen by this heartless brother when Esau was famished. At this desperate moment of weakness, Jacob gives him food and drink in exchange for what amounted to his name being removed from a family will. Who could have guessed that one's own brother could be so heartless, so treacherous, so conniving? When you are that hungry, it is hard to think straight. Esau is not a man with a mushy brain. He simply had a higher regard for what a brother would do, or not do. So it was a bitter pill for Esau to swallow. Yes, a brother sometimes is so greedy, so treacherous, so self-centered, that he will do anything to gain mastery over his own flesh and blood and ultimately gain the wealth he seeks!

Jacob took the blessing that belonged to Esau as the firstborn by treachery and deceit. The bestowal of the blessing by the father was one of the most significant rituals in the Hebrew culture. It is very difficult for us to understand why Isaac, after giving his blessing to the wrong son, could not offer a similar prayer for Esau. Suffice it to say that ancient Hebrew culture understood that whatever was promised could not be revoked. Once spoken, your word was as if the act had already been set in motion and could not be taken back. Just as God spoke at creation and his words became mountains and oceans, so too the spoken word within the human community had a similar power. You could not afterwards say, "I was mistaken about all that we talked about yesterday. Let me clear this up."

In our culture, a man's word may mean nothing whatsoever. We expect promises to be broken at times. Not so with the ancient Hebrew culture. There was no reversing this misdirected blessing, even though it had been deliberately set up by one who went to the trouble of making his arms feel as hairy as his brother's arms to deceive a blind and ailing father who was literally on his deathbed. That is the background.

So what happens to Esau's sworn determination to kill his twin brother? Keep in mind that we are examining this account so as to consider whether respect can be held between two brothers under these extreme circumstances. Esau's threat is indefinitely thwarted. Their mother, Rebekah, learns of Esau's vow to kill his brother. She immediately warns Jacob and sends him off to her brother's estate in Haran, located in northwestern Mesopotamia—a long distance from Esau and Jacob's home (see Gen. 27:42–45). Jacob quietly escapes, and the two brothers do not get to see each other for two decades. Then, finally, the day arrives when the two brothers are to meet. Remember that Esau's last words concerning his brother consisted of a vow to kill him. What will transpire? The two men have not talked to one another for more than twenty years!

We are not given much information about why this meeting was finally to take place, but the text is clear that Jacob was well aware that Esau was not far away and now had the opportunity to carry out his threat. Jacob, who has continued to use deceitfulness and deception all through life, primarily to acquire wealth, now solemnly makes last-minute maneuvers to win his brother's favor.

Consistent with the rest of his life, Jacob tries to bribe or buy his brother's favor and forgiveness with gifts. Because he is now wealthy, he sends ahead of him tremendous gifts hopefully to placate his brother's anger—more than two hundred goats, more than two hundred sheep, thirty camels with their young, and so on. Jacob is so fearful of meeting an angry brother that he divides his huge family into two parties so that at least one group might escape.

So anxious and nervous is Jacob about the outcome of this crucial meeting that he prays to God for his safety and the safety of his family. It is a prayer filled with distress and doubt. "Save me, I pray, from the hand of my brother Esau, for I am afraid he will come and attack me, and also the mothers with their children." (For the entire prayer, see Gen. 32:9–12.) Jacob had reasons for his uneasiness. His guide had let him know that Esau was on his way with four hundred men (see Gen. 32:6).

But who would have guessed the outcome? "When Jacob recognizes his brother Esau some distance away, he bowed down to the ground seven times as he approached his brother" (Gen. 33:3). And then we read one of the most exciting verses in the Bible, "But Esau ran to meet Jacob and embraced him; he threw his arms around his neck and kissed him. And they wept" (Gen. 33:4). After all these years, Jacob is still conniving and calculating. He is still a sleazy brother. His most recent embezzlements had all but ruined Laban, his father-in-law. Now here stands Esau, in tears upon finally finding his brother, his heart filled with love, forgiveness, graciousness, and, yes, trust and respect for Jacob.

As the two clans come together, you see into the hearts of these two men. Esau asks what is the reason for "all these droves I met?" (Gen. 33:8). Jacob meant them as a bribe, so all he can say is, "To find favor in your eyes, my lord." Now note the contrasting response of Esau. "I already have plenty, my brother. Keep what you have for yourself" (Gen. 33:9). Esau addresses Jacob as "my brother," whereas Jacob addresses Esau as "my lord." Jacob keeps insisting that Esau not refuse the hundreds of animals, so Esau accepts the gifts only to please his brother. Esau then offers to escort them to their destination. In response, Jacob gives some lame excuses why it is not convenient or appropriate. When Esau next offers some of his men to protect Jacob's family and their servants and livestock through the remainder of their journey, Jacob does not even have the grace to accept that as an expression of his brother's love.

We have here two very different men. Esau, rich but unpretentious, a family man who can trustingly embrace his brother with tears, despite all of his brother's treachery, lying, and deceitfulness. And Jacob, still maneuvering, still anxious, still plotting against his own family members, still stealing, still buying favor, still conniving, still praying about a brother he fears will attack him—even to the point of killing innocent women! It is a bittersweet story. And one just wonders how Esau's life moved from his angry attempt at murder to a congenial man of character, a gracious soul who could fully forgive and embrace his brother much as the father in Jesus' parable embraces his returning prodigal son. Once again we learn that God's desire is that we fully love and respect each other, even when someone has wronged us. What a wonderful gift Esau brings to his brother—the gift of respect—a gift so much greater than the droves of animals sent forward from Jacob to placate Esau.

These three biblical accounts help us understand how respect works. Respect is not something that is earned. It is an attitude that God wants us to hold consistently before every person we meet. The world works with the opposite assumption—that respect needs to be shown only when we feel it is deserved. The biblical accounts that we have just examined make it abundantly clear that respect is a continuing Christian attitude we hold before all persons. It is to be our attitude toward the homeless person on the street. The politician serving in our district may be engaged in something dishonorable, but when we go to his office with some grievance, we are to be Christlike—that is, we are to speak respectfully. I find nothing in Scripture that allows us to speak disrespectfully to whomever we choose. Respect is the travelling companion that is always faithfully standing beside love and graciousness. As followers of Christ, we are called to offer God's unconditional love and overflowing grace to everyone we meet, and especially to our spouses, treating all with our genuine consideration and utmost respect.

INTEGRATING

How would you score yourself in terms of the respect you show for one another as husband and wife? Let me share with you an experience I had that deepened my understanding of respect and helped me to see that I did not hold my wife with the kind of consideration that the Scriptures illustrate and the life of Jesus exemplifies.

Through the years, I have volunteered with Lend A Hand, an organization that depends upon volunteers working as teams to rebuild houses severely damaged by hurricanes. With Lend A Hand, even the leader or coordinator is a volunteer. You cannot help but admire anyone who accepts without pay the responsibility for overseeing a few dozen volunteers for a week—coordinating travel arrangements for a long road trip; arranging motel accommodations and room assignments; and then enlisting and directing several team leaders who will oversee a project like installing wall board in the entire downstairs of a gutted house! The men and women who assume such mega-responsibilities without even a dollar of pay are rare and remarkable persons.

Among the best of the best were a sister and brother team, Lydia Fehr and Bart Richwine[5]. These two did their homework. They could tell you how long it was until the next break on the bus trip. They could also provide a hard copy of all the contact information for everyone on the bus, direct the driver to the motel or work site as needed, assign projects and work groups, enlist you to provide devotions for a given night, and make sure that all of the tools and materials would be at the work site. Lydia and Bart not only did all that (and much more) with remarkable calm, but they also offered themselves with such pleasantness, good humor, and humility that the entire group enjoyed the week and went home inspired and energized.

Here is what I discovered working as a volunteer under their gifted leadership. I noted that all of the volunteers trusted them with exemplary respect. But some couples, who held the fullest respect and consideration for these fine leaders, *had a somewhat lesser respect for each other as husband and wife.* Some couples would cheerfully accept the most difficult duties from Lydia (such as mucking out a flooded house), but I observed a few husbands being a bit annoyed by or sarcastic with their wives, and wives being less pleasant to or supportive of their husbands. Conversations involving some couples also occasionally revealed a subtle tension or uneasy disagreement that could not be entirely concealed by the couple, even in this congenial fellowship.

From these observations, it was only a short but uncomfortable step to the realization that I was no different in terms of my respect for Joanne. It was simply less evident because Joanne was back home, a thousand miles away. The discovery was painful, since I thought I was above average in my role as husband. I had to admit that I could readily remember times that very month when I had had more than a trace of impatience or disdain in my choice of words or a tone of criticism or sarcasm in my voice over something that now escaped me as a worthy issue. What I could clearly remember was my attitude, my disrespect.

When my turn came to lead devotions one evening, I decided I would share my personal struggle with this issue, guided by Scripture.

Confession is an amazing thing—it makes the listener more able to hear! We are touched to the core of our being by an honest confession. Less than an hour after devotions, one husband had delivered flowers from a local florist to the entrance of his wife's tent. Three cheers! Two other men walked a half-mile and returned with sundaes for their wives, to show their love and new intentions. I have never seen such tangible results from any of my sermons or devotions as I did that night!

As for myself, I went home determined, with God's help, to treat my wife and family with the fullness of respect that we see in the life of Christ our Lord. If you want to be aware of how much you show respect—or disrespect—to those closest to you, be aware of the tone of your voice and those words or glances that convey sarcasm, however subtle. Be on the lookout for words of criticism, which many of us frequently pour out, but so poorly receive. Put downs, whether mild or harsh, and our tendencies to belittle are signals to alert us of a lack of respect on our part.

I find that my own moments of disrespect occur over minor decisions. Being respectful is easy when we are dealing with weightier matters such as Aunt Evie's lung cancer or when we are comforting a sister or brother at a funeral. But be on your guard when you are discussing what features you need on a new refrigerator or deciding whether to repaint or trash the picket fence that no longer is needed for the children or the dog. We may find ourselves saying peevishly, "I cannot believe you would just trash all the memories we have of our children playing out there in the yard!" Or we might respond sarcastically, "So because you have this silly sentimentality, I have to commit two weekends of my time repainting a mile of fencing!"

There is nothing wrong with having different views of a problem—preferring an earth-tone color for the master bedroom over a light, sunny yellow. What is wrong is our attitude of condescension that says in effect—"Anyone who would prefer an earth-tone color for their bedroom is a bit daffy. The bedroom should be a romantic place and painted a passionate color, like magenta!" Deciding what color we are going to paint a room may seem like a small thing, but apparently it is more important to us than we think, seeing how we handle the discussion almost combatively.

I believe that there is a close correspondence between our disrespect and our self-esteem. If I plant the new tree exactly where *I* want it planted, my ego is satisfied. Unfortunately, we at times see the choice as a matter of winning or losing. And we do not like to lose! We need to learn how to discuss the pros and cons candidly and cheerfully, so that we arrive at the best decision possible—together—a decision that is ultimately exciting for both partners.

A Prayer

Lord of all, I confess that I keep at a distance those who are disrespectful of me, yet I am so often guilty of treating my own spouse disrespectfully. Those words of disrespect, subtly conveyed in the impatient tone of my voice or in words of hurtful criticism or in eyes turned to the ceiling, have cost us much of our warmth and intimacy. Considered singly, they do not seem to weigh in that heavily. But over the course of months and years, they have become a logjam of hurt, and we are no longer able to convey our deepest love from one heart to the other. Lord, it is no wonder that Zacchaeus became a new man after meeting you. Never had he been so welcomed into the heart of another, with not a single word of condemnation, and not the smallest hint of judgment! Lord Jesus, help me be that way with my spouse. Help me through your indwelling spirit to be more aware of my choice of words, the sarcasm in my voice, and the put-downs that are never funny. Grant me patience, because I have no right to expect this to change our marriage instantly. After all, Lord, I have been doing this to her (or him) for too many years. Make me, day by day, a more loving and sensitive man (or woman). In Jesus' name. Amen.

Three Questions

1. Why do so many couples fail to regard their spouses with at least as much respect as they offer to their work associates or golfing partners?
2. Can you identify your own pattern of disrespect? Do you make fun of your mate in the presence of your friends in order

to make your point about his (her) weight, smoking habits, spending sprees, or whatever issue bothers you? Or do you tend to come in like a stealth fighter plane, seizing the perfect opportunity to voice your irritation, giving your words maximum weight? Do you see a pattern in your disrespectful attitude?

3.   Do you find that disrespect usually is responded to with disrespect? How could you begin to break that cycle this coming week?

INSIGHTS

Fourscore and seven years ago our fathers brought forth on this continent a new nation, conceived in liberty, and dedicated to the proposition that all men are created equal.

—Abraham Lincoln

I want to be the white man's brother, not his brother-in-law.

—Martin Luther King, Jr.

He causes his sun to rise on the evil and the good, and sends rain on the righteous and the unrighteous.

—Matt. 5:45

I realize that patriotism is not enough. I must have no hatred or bitterness toward anyone.

—Edith Cavell (her last words)

To speak ill of others is a dishonest way of praising ourselves.

—Will Durant

A great many people think they are thinking when they are merely rearranging their prejudices.

—William James

Unless we are willing to help a person overcome his faults, there is little value in pointing them out.

—Robert J. Hastings

The essential corruption of racial segregation is not that it is supported by lies but that people believe the lies.

—Harry Golden

The arrows of sarcasm are barbed with contempt.

—Washington Gladden

The ground is level at the foot of the cross.

—Anonymous

CHAPTER EIGHT

Whatever you do, work at it with all your heart, as working for the Lord, not for men, since you know that you will receive an inheritance from the Lord as a reward. It is the Lord Christ you are serving.

—Col. 3:23–24

ƒERVING GOD
ƒIDE BY ƒIDE

INTERPERSONAL

Joanne and I have always seen ourselves as a team. When we "graduated" out of our high-school youth fellowship, there was little in our modest-sized congregation for young adults. So we created a group called "Ambassadors," using Paul's word in Second Corinthians 5:20. One of the early joys in our marriage was hosting and enabling this Bible study and fellowship for young adults.

When God called me into the ministry, we prayed for about nine months to be sure this was God's calling and not our own desire. Because we had married by that time, we instinctively knew that God had to speak to both of our hearts, and not just to one of us. Joanne felt the call as strongly as I did, but when friends asked us about how God was leading us in the matter, Joanne would often reply playfully, "Well, Bob has his suitcases all packed and waiting at the front door, but I am still praying!"

It was important to have that call confirmed in both of us because we would have to sell our first home in a Baltimore suburb and complete seven years of higher education. Joanne saw her call largely as giving support through her full-time work with a telephone company so that we could maintain ourselves financially for a long-term run.

Those seven years were challenging, at times bringing us to tears, but we persevered because we both felt God's calling to do this. We were absolutely convinced that God had placed this on our hearts, and so we never saw giving up as an option, even when our house did not sell, causing financial pressure from the very first month.

When I graduated *cum laude* from Westminster College in New Wilmington, Pennsylvania, the first person in either of our families to earn a college degree, we saw it as an achievement that we had teamed. The same was true for seminary. When I graduated from Princeton, our family and friends understood clearly that it was a joint endeavor every step of the way. When my church presented me with a handsome clerical robe as a part of the celebration of becoming ordained, I bought my wife a beautiful gold coat with black fur trim as one way of thanking her for sharing in our preparation for ministry.

Through thirty-five years of pastorates, each congregation that called me came to know eventually that they had in reality called a couple—two people with different gifts, not in competition with each other, but both of us committed to using our gifts to build up faith in Jesus Christ in the lives of our people.

Now that we are retired, we continue to serve God as a team. If Joanne becomes sick, I cover her Meals on Wheels run. She does the same for me. Twice a year I volunteer with Lend A Hand, traveling to Florida, Mississippi, or Iowa by bus to help rebuild homes severely damaged by hurricanes and flooding. During the nine days I am away, I will work about *forty hours* finishing drywall. During those same nine days Joanne will do about *eighty hours* of work covering my absence by doing babysitting without my help, keeping up with weeds, paying bills, and all that goes into maintaining a home and caring for family and friends. Right now, as I am writing this book, Joanne is doing all the word processing. Side by side, we are still serving God as a team.

INSPIRING

After this, Paul left Athens and went to Corinth. There he met a Jew named Aquila, a native of Pontus, who had recently come from Italy with his wife Priscilla because Claudius had ordered all the

Jews to leave Rome. Paul went to see them, and because he was a tentmaker as they were, he stayed and worked with them. Paul stayed on in Corinth for some time. Then he left the brothers and sailed for Syria, accompanied by Priscilla and Aquila. They arrived at Ephesus, where Paul left Priscilla and Aquila. . . . Meanwhile a Jew named Apollos, a native of Alexandria, came to Ephesus. He was a learned man, with a thorough knowledge of the Scriptures. He had been instructed in the way of the Lord, and he spoke with great fervor and taught about Jesus accurately, though he knew only the baptism of John. He began to speak boldly in the synagogue.

When Priscilla and Aquila heard him, they invited him to their home and explained to him the way of God more adequately.
—see Acts 18:1–3, 18–19, 24–26

Greet Priscilla and Aquila, my fellow workers in Christ Jesus. They risked their lives for me. Not only me but all the churches of the Gentiles are grateful to them. Greet also the church that meets at their house.
—Rom. 16:3–5

IMAGINING

One House in Oakville

(Dedicated to the many volunteers who have served in Oakville, Iowa, rebuilding homes ravaged by the Iowa River flooding of 2008)

The good Samaritan
Just one man
One compassionate man
Willing to stop on a dangerous road to help a badly beaten up
    traveler
Just one man desperately needing help
Not able to help himself
Just one donkey to get him to the inn
Just one promise to pay for his care
The good Samaritan
Christ's gold standard for caring
One compassionate man

Just one house on River Road
Ten of us worked all week on this one house.
A house badly beaten up, first by fire, then by flood,
Its window frames blackened by the licking flames,
The first floor later flooded by the swelling, bulging Iowa River,
Carrying so much rain water that it could not make its final torturous
    curve before emptying its piled up waters into the mighty
    Mississippi
So the rushing, gushing waters took their own straightway shortcut to
    the Mississippi,
Overland and straight down River Road,
Transforming the little town of Oakville into a lake of wild waters.
The River Road signposts still standing just above the water line,
Startling evidence of the depth of these rising, rushing, and ravaging
    flood waters,
Delivering tons of mud into the once comfortable living room and
    dining room of the Ford family,
And bringing with it destruction, discouragement, and despair,
And the Fords' family decision to leave mud-encased Oakville—
The painful decision of one overwhelmed family
Just one family desperately needing help,
Not able to help themselves.

Just one bus pulling into Oakville
Just a couple dozen volunteers from Pennsylvania
Willing to give just one week of work amid a dismal landscape of
    destruction,
A miniature world without grass.
A team of twelve measuring and cutting drywall on Monday and
    Tuesday;
Back again on Wednesday and Thursday measuring and hanging
    drywall;
Hanging and finishing drywall all week.
Metal tapes stretched out to get a careful measurement with a clink,
Then squealing back into their little house.
Pencils quietly record each figure on a scrap of studding.
A saw screams through its cuts.
Strong arms lift the sheet of drywall carefully into place.

Impatient power drills screech screws into marked studs.
Loving hands patiently and painstakingly apply compound and
      taping to every joint in every room,
While trained hands finish a mile of ceiling corners with unhurried
      precision.
The finishing touch of corner beads on doorways gives a new house
      look!
And all the while walls are smoothed out by hissing sanding blocks.
Ten rooms transformed into beautiful living space!
Just one busload of volunteers
Just one week of work
Just one house in Oakville.

The Ford family—
A young family of five—
So disheartened and down that they nearly left town,
But now are filled with hope.
Larry brought his three-year-old daughter by to see
      her "new" room,
Ready to be painted in her favorite color.
We enjoyed seeing her excitement,
And the joy expressed in her dancing eyes!
Just one little girl in Oakville
Just one father in a family of five
Just one busload of people
Just one week of work
Just one family desperately needing help
Just one house in Oakville.

                              —Bob Unverzagt, Lend A Hand volunteer

INTERPRETING

Priscilla and Aquila are mentioned by name five times in the New
Testament. Except for one instance, Priscilla's name is always first.
The apostle Paul refers to Priscilla and Aquila twice (see Rom. 16:3–5
and 2 Tim. 4:19) and provides some specific and compelling infor-
mation about them. The gospel writer Luke refers to them in The
Acts of the Apostles twice as "Priscilla and Aquila," and once with

Aquila's name first, probably because Luke is telling his readers how Paul and Aquila first met—Priscilla not then with him.

It is highly irregular for the man not to be named first in first-century culture. Was Priscilla a more socially adept person who had a vivacious personality that placed her more in the foreground of Paul and Luke's memories? Was Aquila a quieter type with his own gifts, perhaps known and appreciated for his ability to get the task done even though it may have been a strategy or vision of his wife? Since the Bible rarely names couples, our curiosity about Priscilla and Aquila is piqued! We wonder about their marriage, their faith in Christ, how they went about hosting the church that met in their house, and their leadership style in the growing first-century church as they apparently served God side by side.

There are several couples with whom Joanne and I enjoy significant friendships—couples who have authentic and exemplary Christian-based marriages that inspire and encourage us. Their oneness in Christ is so strong and real that both husband and wife come to mind whenever either name is mentioned. Even death has not changed this. A couple of them are now widows, but my thoughts of them as a couple always recall both—husband and wife still standing side by side! I get the feeling from the Scriptures that Priscilla and Aquila were such a couple. (How many couples do you know that have names that rhyme!)

There are three reasons why we can speculate that their marriage was vital and strong with their faith rooted in Jesus Christ. First, the church met in their home (see Rom. 16:3–5). There were no church buildings in the first century, so the believers gathered in various homes. This commitment not only singles this couple out for their gift of hospitality, but more especially for their courage. The first century church faced great persecution from its earliest years, and any Christian who dared to host groups of believers had to have considerable courage and a deep faith in God. Such men and women found themselves in much the same hostile and dangerous environment as the Jews faced in Germany during the Hitler regime of World War II.

The author of Hebrews sums up the costliness of first century faith in Christ with jarring and straightforward language, telling us how some "were tortured and refused to be released, so that they might gain a better resurrection. Some faced jeers and flogging, while still others were chained and put in prison. They were stoned; they were sawed in two; they were put to death by the sword. They went about in sheepskins and goatskins, destitute, persecuted and mistreated" (Heb. 11:35–37).

Priscilla and Aquila lived in Ephesus, a major city with a great many of its citizens believing in the goddess Artemis. Citizens of Ephesus saw the infant Christian faith as a threat to their own culture and religion. (See Acts 19, especially verses 17–34.) Priscilla herself had fled from her family home in Rome as a result of an edict published by the Emperor Claudius, ordering all Jews to leave Rome (see Acts 18:2). Those who chose "The Way" and became known as Christians had a joyous and stirring story about a gracious and loving God who came into the world as a man to help us understand the nature of God. Through his death he freely offered forgiveness and redemption, and through his resurrection he freely offered to all victory over death and the gift of eternal life! Christianity possessed a treasure in its remarkable message of good news that was difficult to compete with in terms of the joy, forgiveness, and hope offered by a deity who was generous and loving. Nevertheless, in such circumstances, a couple hosting a Christian group had to be courageous. They needed a strong marriage to risk their lives by hosting in their home a new faith viewed by many as a danger to the existing religion.

Second, Priscilla and Aquila in some way had risked their lives for Paul's sake. Paul mentions their names near the end of Romans, along with about thirty others whom Paul remembered. There he thanks them for somehow saving his life. "Greet Priscilla and Aquila, my fellow workers in Christ Jesus. They risked their lives for me" (Rom. 16:3–4). They had very likely helped with hiding Paul after he had been opposed or attacked by enemies of The Way. When a person risks his or her life for another, the situation is usually one of urgency. You normally will not have three weeks to hold committee meetings before you decide to act!

Priscilla and Aquila were attuned to one another's hearts. They did not have to excuse themselves for twenty or thirty minutes to discuss whether they could respond as one. A healthy, joyous marriage flows out of oneness of heart, mind, and soul as well as the oneness of physical connection. In whatever way Aquila and Priscilla risked their lives for the apostle Paul, I would guess that at the end of the day neither one said to the other, "Dearest, you could have had both of us killed today by stepping into that dangerous situation just to protect one person."

I have been bandying Parkinson's disease for over ten years, but it does not cause conflict with Joanne when I volunteer for a week of rebuilding homes in Mississippi and travel more than a thousand miles before I begin the eight-hour workdays. We are of one mind to make and keep the commitment, even though it might be somewhat rigorous for me because the disease has reduced my stamina and endurance. Joanne never says to me, "Bob, you're really being foolish doing this with your Parkinson's. If something happened to you, think about what that could mean for me." Instead, she chooses to say, "I really admire what you're doing, and you will be in my prayers every day." We are of one mind and purpose—serving God together.

Third, Priscilla and Aquila knew how to serve God in unison—quickly complementing one another, supporting one another, and working intuitively as a team. Many married persons seem immediately to come up with at least one or two reasons why whatever their spouse wants to do cannot be done. If you want to really surprise your mate, the next time he/she wants to do something (take the family vacation a month earlier; renovate the laundry room; team teach a seminar on parenting adolescents, etc.) give her/him as quickly as you can two solid reasons why you think it's a great idea! She/he will be startled and will love you for it.

When Priscilla and Aquila heard Apollos preach, they realized that while he was very knowledgeable and accurate about the new Christian faith, there were many important segments of Christ's ministry that he seemed to be without. Then we read in Acts 18:26, "When Priscilla and Aquila heard him, they invited him to their home and explained to him the way of God more adequately." It does not say that Priscilla and Aquila found a secluded spot to talk over how they felt about inviting a stranger to their house, knowing they had left their kitchen in a mess. Priscilla and Aquila enjoyed adventuring together. They found excitement and joy in doing spontaneous and purposeful things. Because of the depth of their love, they were confident that together they could expand Apollos's knowledge of Christ, and consequently share in a meaningful experience, side by side serving Christ their Lord.

INTEGRATING

Several years ago, Joanne and I became separated at the end of a worship experience as we were greeting our friends. I happened to meet a new couple who were visiting our church for the first time. I knew our day was free, so after talking with the newcomers, I asked them if they would enjoy going out to dinner to get acquainted. They quickly replied saying they would enjoy doing that, after merely glancing at one another knowingly. I then had the opportunity to introduce them to my wife and gently filled her in about dining as a foursome after church.

The four of us went out to a restaurant together and had a great time for about two hours before parting. Joanne never glared at me or felt like she had been left outside of the decision. The connection probably would never have happened if I had to first confer with Joanne in a corner somewhere before extending our warm invitation. Observing our need for a check-in with one another, the visiting couple may have felt that they were imposing on us and graciously said no. It turned out to be the beginning of a close and enduring friendship with Tom and Nancy Kitzmiller[6]. Why? Was it because the four of us had just enough of the qualities Priscilla and Aquila possessed, namely, a growing oneness that enabled us to trust one another intuitively. Joanne knew that whatever I had committed us to was something that she would most likely enjoy. She could be flexible and spontaneous, responding affirmatively and warmly to Tom and Nancy.

This invitation seems like a simple exchange—an invitation to lunch that was graciously accepted. But any one of the four of us could have killed this spontaneous act for any number of reasons: feeling hurt because we were left out of the decision; lacking flexibility; not feeling in the mood to meet newcomers; having had a spat at breakfast that was not fully resolved; not having enough trust to warmly support the husband's judgment; feeling angry about the financial aspect of the invitation; and so on.

As we learn how to love one another more deeply, we depend less on "rules" or even tacit understandings. Consider how Paul instructs the Christians in Rome. "But now, by dying to what once bound us, we have been released from the law so that we serve in the new way of the Spirit, and not in the old way of the written code" (Rom. 7:6). Because we know that our mate really loves us and will always sensitively consider our needs, we are able to assume some risk. We will feel more secure to enter into a new experience in serving others. The experience of serving will often lead to new joys as well as significant friendships.

Serving God harmoniously as a couple does not mean that each partner needs to be excited about the same ministry. Most of the volunteers I have served beside over the past several years come alone. Their spouses stay at home to care for the kids and the family's domestic needs, making the volunteer's work possible. There were a spattering of couples—perhaps three or four in a group of thirty to thirty-five volunteers. But whether one spouse remained at home, or the couple served together, both husband and wife needed to appreciate what the other was doing and cheerfully run with it, affirming both the integrity of the ministry and their mate's week-long participation in it.

To summarize, a careful examination of Priscilla and Aquila's ministry to others suggests that a marriage can be enriched by taking on adventurous commitments that bless the lives of others and often require some risk or sacrifice. The scripture passages that we earlier examined suggest the following principles and qualities:

- *Your level of trust for one another has to be as deep as the commitment to serve is difficult or dangerous.* Priscilla and Aquila were able to face challenging, life-threatening situations courageously because they had learned how to trust one another deeply. Both knew clearly what the other could handle in terms of their own personal security, their level of risk, their willingness to sacrifice, their faith in God to protect them, and the depth of their desire to help another person.

- *You need to pay attention to your partner's unique gifts and capacities so that he/she will have a measure of confidence and reassurance that he/she can make a contribution to the ministry, especially if it is a new experience.* If you are feeding the homeless at an inner city mission, you both need to feel comfortable greeting, talking with, and encouraging people who are at a radically different place in life than you are. They also need to be treated with love and dignity. Will you both feel reasonably safe walking streets that may be occupied with drug dealers, homeless persons, or soliciting prostitutes? It takes years of growing, interacting, and awareness to build an accurate personal knowledge of your mate's gifts, needs, and strengths so that you are attuned to one another and can choose a particular service to glorify God together, in unison, as one.

- *You need to respect your spouse's feelings when she/he feels anxious about some form of service that you feel passionate about.* You may be excited about a ministry that meets with men in prison to encourage and mentor them. You may also feel that your wife is a gifted conversationalist with experience in tutoring, as well as being very positive about life. In your eyes, she is a prime candidate for ministry to women in prison. But if she feels too anxious or fearful and is concerned that she be around to raise your two beautiful daughters, you need to respect her needs and her decision and back off. You do not want to push her into a ministry that would cause her sleepless nights. The reciprocal situation is equally a concern. The wife needs to accept and respect her husband's limits, and not take them lightly. Any ministry we choose to do should be a source of fulfillment and joy, not a contributor to stress and worry.

The capacity of a couple to thoughtfully serve God in a particular ministry as a team is a significant measure of a couple's maturity, both in terms of their marriage and their personal faith. While the maturity may take years of effort to acquire, once reached, it brings to us a deeper and more lasting joy than we could ever have by shopping at our favorite mall or playing a round of golf together.

A Prayer

Most generous God, you have given us an infinite array of gifts to enjoy. Among them, almost hidden by the breathtaking color and brightness of the others, is the shy and unobtrusive gift of service. Never clamoring for attention, it waits patiently for us to find it with mature eyes. And once we have found it, we also find one of the deepest of joys, as well as one of the best teachers of love. Lord, grant us the courage and freedom to take that decisive step that opens up for us that deep and significant practice in the life of our Lord that serves one another in love. Guide us as husband and wife to a point of service that excites and captivates our spirits and perfectly uses our gifts and strengths to do it with joy. And may this new experience in self-giving increase our joy in you and in each other. In the name of him who stooped to wash his disciples' feet, Jesus our Lord. Amen.

Three Questions

1. Think of a time in your life when you cared for another person (or persons), bringing them support, encouragement, or practical help. How did you feel about that experience? Was it exciting, frustrating, fulfilling, intimidating, a source of joy, etc.? Why?
2. Thoughtfully identify two or three skills, gifts, or abilities that are presently a part of your life, and which God could possibly use in some form of service to others?
3. How could a husband and wife with very little experience in Christian service creatively go about finding or choosing an arena of service that they could enjoy together—a service that was challenging but not intimidating or overwhelming? Be as specific as you can.

INSIGHTS

The sole meaning of life is to serve humanity.

—Leo Tolstoy

It is high time that the ideal of success should be replaced by the ideal of service.

—Albert Einstein

The greatest pleasure I know is to do a good action by stealth and have it found out by accident.

—Charles Lamb

If one were in a rapture like St. Paul, and there was a sick man needing help, I think it would be best to throw off the rapture and show love by service to the needy.

—Meister Eckhart

Somewhere out there is a unique place for you to help others—a unique role for you to fill, that only you can fill.

—Thomas Kinkade

A Christian man is the most free lord of all, and subject to none; a Christian man is the most dutiful servant of all, and subject to everyone.

—Martin Luther

Do not use your freedom to indulge the sinful nature; rather, serve one another in love. The entire law is summed up in a single command: "Love your neighbor as yourself."

—Gal. 5:13–14

Take that gift God has entrusted to you, and use it in the service of Christ and your fellow men. He will make it glow and shine like the very stars of heaven.

—John Sutherland Bonnell

I expect to pass through life but once. If, therefore, there be any kindness I can show, or any good thing I can do for any fellow being, let me do it now . . . as I shall not pass this way again.

—William Penn

CHAPTER NINE

We are hard pressed on every side, but not crushed; perplexed, but not in despair; persecuted, but not abandoned; struck down, but not destroyed.

—2 Cor. 4:8–9

ſETBACKſ AND ſUFFERING

INTERPERSONAL

In 2004, I signed up with Pennsylvania-based Lend A Hand to do my first week of volunteer work in Florida, rebuilding homes that had been severely damaged by a hard-hitting hurricane. I was excited about this new experience. I had volunteered for Habitat for Humanity workdays for years, but this was my first nine-day experience, traveling by bus with about thirty others from Pennsylvania. The two-day trip down was over a thousand miles. When we arrived at our host church, we unloaded all our gear and found our assigned rooms for sleeping.

I then found a chair in the foyer and sat down to relax and read the Sunday newspaper. A friend came by and offered me his cell phone with "free minutes" to call my wife. I was thrilled and called her at once. Joanne responded by saying with some urgency in her voice, "Thanks for calling me back—I guess you got my message. We have had an emergency here. I fell at a restaurant, and paramedics dining almost next to me immediately came to my aid. The short version is that I have a badly fractured wrist. It has been temporarily casted. How are things there?"

While I was bused through Georgia, Joanne was being taken by ambulance to the hospital! She had not called me earlier because she wanted to wait until she could better assess her situation. I was of course disappointed about having to return home immediately and talked the situation over to see what would be best.

Our daughter Sandy had already driven almost one hundred miles to see what she could do to help. Her family of four came despite the fact that three of them were extremely sick, and the girls were not quite four years old. For them, it was a no-brainer—Dad would return home! Joanne is no wimp when it comes to a tough situation, and after discussing it for at least fifteen minutes, she insisted that I stay for the first workday on Monday. We agreed that I would call her Monday night to see how she was managing. She would need surgery on her right hand and would require three pins placed by a specialist. She would probably be scheduled for the procedure later in the week. She urged me to stay for Tuesday's workday, and we would check in with each other nightly. Due to their sickness, Sandy and her family had to return home, but Joanne was managing with one hand amazingly well.

Joanne was finally scheduled for surgery on Friday morning, so on Thursday evening we decided I would fly home early Friday morning. Her brother Jim would provide transportation for her to meet me at the airport and we would go on to the hospital together. The three of us arrived at the hospital thirty minutes before surgery. She had almost single-handedly enabled me to fulfill my volunteer week by her perseverance and determination.

As it turned out, it rained so hard on our last workday in Florida that our entire Lend A Hand team could not work any of their Friday hours. And Joanne, who is the ultimate coupon clipper, had electronically ticketed my flight home using our frequent flyer miles!

How do you handle the setbacks and disappointments in your marriage? Can you sacrifice attention to yourself to make a bad situation a testimony of God's empowering?

Inspiring

> But now, this is what the LORD says—he who created you, O Jacob, he who formed you, O Israel: "Fear not, for I have redeemed you; I have summoned you by name; you are mine. When you pass through the waters, I will be with you; and when

you pass through the rivers, they will not sweep over you. When you walk through the fire, you will not be burned; the flames will not set you ablaze. For I am the LORD, your God, the Holy One of Israel, your Savior; . . . Do not be afraid, for I am with you; . . ."

—Isa. 43:1–3, 5

Though the fig tree does not bud and there are no grapes on the vines, though the olive crop fails and the fields produce no food, though there are no sheep in the pen and no cattle in the stalls, yet I will rejoice in the LORD, I will be joyful in God my Savior. The Sovereign LORD is my strength; he makes my feet like the feet of a deer, he enables me to go on the heights.

—Hab. 3:17–19

IMAGINING

Lord, I Have a Few Questions

Lord, I have a few questions.

I know that you love us as your children, but why does a Down-syndrome child have to go through her first six years of schooling always struggling with the fact that every other girl and boy in her class is far more capable than she is?

And, Lord, why does a frail woman in her nineties, crippled for decades with painful arthritis, have to be bedridden for three years and routinely left alone for a few hours at a time because her family is too poor to give up one of their jobs so that a family member could sit with her and provide companionship, conversation, comfort, and care?

Lord, I have a few questions on my heart.

Why did my sister, Jean, and I have to go through nearly three of our pre-school years without our mom around because she was in isolation at a distant sanitarium battling tuberculosis? And why did she have to go through the removal of one lung in her early twenties just a few days after her best friend died as a result of the same surgery?

And why must a young girl, still in her adolescence, have to deal with being an unwed mother, deserted by a young boy who is no longer "in love with her," and so is left with the burden of raising the child alone—the whole incident not really her fault since her parents and her church failed to teach her your beautiful purpose for her sexuality?

Lord, I deeply respect you, but I need answers to some nagging questions.

I know you have immense power to jettison a planet like Saturn into orbit as easily as a marble propelled from a boy's thumb, so why would you not use the tiniest fraction of your power to stop a cement truck with failed brakes from careening through a stop sign and killing a teenaged son whose parents, following him home, had to helplessly and painfully witness his death?

And, gracious Lord, how could it be wrong to ask you to step in for a second to prevent a father from backing his car out of his garage and unknowingly into his toddler son, a fatal accident that is still tormenting his heart—especially because his wife will not forgive him even after some twenty years?

Lord, I have talked these things over at great length with friends on many occasions, but they are still questions without answers.

For instance, why does a loving family have to go through the terrible pain of knowing that a close family member took his life without leaving a clue as to his struggle?

Lord, you know the questions that are on my heart before I ask them.

Such as, why would you allow a disabled elderly woman to die in a fire that quickly filled her house with a blinding, disorienting smoke while her husband, at her encouragement, attended Sunday morning worship at their church?

And our entire family is still aching over this one—why does our daughter, Sandy, have to deal with the diagnosis of an aggressive breast cancer just a few days before she was excited to begin her fourth year of homeschooling her eight-year-old twin daughters, Charis and Syd?

Lord, I have a few questions on my heart

(All of the above situations are actual occurrences within families of believers to whom the author has been a pastor.)

INTERPRETING

God does not seem to have any problems with suffering in the same way we do. After all, God the Father suffered through the excruciating ordeal of his only begotten Son's death on the cross for the redemption of the world. "When they hurled their insults at him, he did not retaliate; when he suffered, he made no threats; . . . by his wounds you have been healed" (1 Peter 2:23–24). So one could even argue that suffering can be positive, accomplishing enormous blessings for untold millions.

The Bible, more than once, suggests that our own sufferings can be life giving, leading us somehow to a greater depth of character and spiritual maturity. After the apostle Paul tells us that we can rejoice because Christ has enabled us to have peace with God through his death, he then adds, "Not only so, *but we also rejoice in our sufferings,* because we know that suffering produces perseverance; perseverance, character; and character, hope" (Rom. 5:3–4, emphasis mine).

I do not believe Paul was suggesting that there is a mechanical law in which:

1. Suffering creates perseverance;
2. Perseverance in turn creates character;
3. Character unfailingly creates hope.

Rather, I think the apostle sees this in a more fluid sense, analogous to a rock falling into a serene lake, producing rings of ripples. You cannot really tell where one ring starts or another ring ends. So too, if we examine our past sufferings, we may see that they somehow increased our perseverance and patience, somehow deepened our character, and brought us closer to Christ. And your growing relationship in Christ (over months or even years) may have awakened within you the glorious glow of hope that is always expectantly lifting your eyes toward God.

If we never had to deal with suffering or difficulties, we would have no way of knowing how much we can endure, or for that matter, how one can feel a sense of hope after having passed through one of the most painful experiences in life. A quadriplegic like Joni Eareckson Tada knows what the human spirit can endure because God has guided her into a deeper and deeper personal faith and sense of hope that is stronger and more enduring than that which she had in her heart before her "tragic" diving accident occurred.

Our scripture selection from Isaiah 43 emphasizes God's unfailing presence in our lives as we pass through our most overwhelming experiences. The prophet Isaiah is likely imagining a wilderness pioneer crossing a river with belongings on his back. The waters first come up to his waist, then to his chest. He begins to feel the full strength of the river's power. Then God says, "When you pass through the waters, I will be with you; and when you pass through the rivers, they will not sweep over you. . . . Do not be afraid, for I am with you" (Isa. 43:2, 5). God never abandons us. He is with us all the time, endlessly. We never have to go it alone.

Note also that the prophet does not say, "*Should you ever* pass through the waters, I will be with you." That would imply that there is at least a remote possibility that one might go through his entire life without ever experiencing suffering or setbacks. Instead, Isaiah assumes that all of us will from time to time feel the burden of unwanted pain or suffering, so he says, "*When* you pass through the waters. . . . *When* you walk through the fire . . . do not be afraid, for I am with you" (Isa. 43:2, emphasis mine). We should expect times of setback in our marriages because setbacks are a significant part of life in this broken, fallen, and imperfect world. And yet, even though times of suffering may be unavoidable and even inevitable, we can be comforted because we never have to walk alone.

The apostle Paul also offers a very similar insight into suffering that very closely parallels the content of the Isaiah passage. "We are hard pressed on every side, but not crushed; perplexed, but not in despair; persecuted, but not abandoned; struck down, but not destroyed" (2 Cor. 4:8–9).

Several weeks ago I was driving up a ramp to get on the interstate when I noticed an insect on my windshield. As my car accelerated to fifty, then sixty, the little bug slowly but ingeniously repositioned itself so that its wings allowed the wind to pass over his body aerodynamically while also pressing his body more flush to the windshield. The wind actually helped the nearly weightless tiny creature to hang on until I reached the stop sign at the next interchange. The bug had endured sixty miles per hour winds, but at least it was not "crushed" as an insect would be if it randomly hit the windshield at the same speed. In a similar way, God chooses to develop our endurance and character through our difficult and challenging experiences that may at times cause us to feel "hard-pressed," "perplexed," or even "struck down." But because God is with us, we are not "crushed," we are not "in despair," we are not "destroyed."

Let us be honest. If life were always perfect, if nothing ever went wrong, if the skies were always sunny, if we never came across a rotten apple, if we never broke an arm or leg, if we were never low on money, if we never had any health problems, if we never had cause for tears, you can be sure of it—we would all become bratty, spoiled, and obnoxious children. So God sees our obstacles and hardships and difficulties as a means of teaching us the most valuable insights and discoveries of a lifetime. Pain may mysteriously make us more compassionate. A cancer diagnosis may nudge us to rethink what is truly important. The loss of a job for several months may become a blessing as we use the many long hours of silence to re-examine who we are and why God has put us here. This is not to say that suffering always makes us better people. But it does appear that it significantly increases our chances.

Besides, if God lavished upon us only good all the days of our lives, wouldn't it "pay" to worship such a God? If I could get 60 percent gain annually from my investments by placing them in

Divine Securities, Inc., why would I want to put them anywhere else? Making such a decision would not even sharpen my reasoning! If a farmer in Iowa never had to deal with drought conditions, but always had just the right amount of sun and rainfall, would not faith and trust in God be obvious? But under such perfect and generous conditions, what would you need to do to be regarded as courageous or persevering? You would not even be able to express goodness or kindness toward your neighbors since they would be living in the same sumptuous plenty.

What a different picture of faith Habakkuk offers. Listen to his personal statement of faith in God after having gone through the worst imaginable nightmare in farming losses: "Though the fig tree does not bud and there are no grapes on the vines, though the olive crop fails and the fields produce no food, though there are no sheep in the pen and no cattle in the stalls, *yet I will rejoice in the LORD, I will be joyful in God my Savior*" (Hab. 3:17–18, emphasis mine). There is an expression of faith that is inspiring. There you have true joy embodied in a life going through the wringer. When we are hard pressed, God does not disappear from us. Instead, he wants to comfort and empower us. He wants to make our faith in him more vigorous. "The Sovereign Lord is my strength," says Habakkuk.

This extraordinary servant of God did not sit on a tree stump, his head slumped in his hands, sulking and complaining. Rather, he testifies to an amazing God who is far greater than our sufferings. Habakkuk does not say that God somehow drags him out of his problems and enables him somehow to survive. Not at all! He tells us that God, "makes my feet like the feet of a deer, he enables me to go to the heights" (Hab. 3:19). That is to say, God gives him a lightness of step. He could still tackle a mountain. Are you aware that God is still with you as you walk through disappointments and setbacks in your marriage? Have you searched for clues and signs of his unfailing presence and caring? Or are you assuming that you are all alone and trying to make things better using your own best thinking or the "good advice" of friends?

A few years ago, when our grandchildren were three years old, we had an Easter egg hunt in our back yard. Because some of the children were so little, those who hid the eggs put them in obvious places. I can still see one of our littlest toddlers nearly stepping on a yellow egg that was placed beside a couple of dandelions of matching color! She walked over it and kept on going! Those of us who noticed smiled. It is not quite as amusing when we as adults do the same thing spiritually. God is right there with us, as near as the ground we are walking on, yet we walk on without making any connection at all.

INTEGRATING

As you look back over the years, would you say that your times of greatest growth and your best seasons of experiencing nearness to God were when you received a significant promotion in your career, or bought a beautiful new van that was fully equipped, or enjoyed a ten-day vacation as a couple exploring the pristine islands of Hawaii? Or did you mature spiritually and draw closer and more trustingly to Christ as your Lord as a result of being unemployed for more than a year, or when you faced the anxiety of a cancer diagnosis and endured a regimen of chemotherapy or radiation treatments, or was it when your husband or son was wounded on one of the world's battlefields and came home with a disability?

The apostle Paul experienced many forms of suffering as a result of presenting the gospel. Here is his personal list of the events that really enriched his life, filling it with vitality and passion and solidly connecting him with the God of the universe. "As servants of God, we commend ourselves in every way [Paul means that their lives are validated in the following experiences]; in great endurance; in troubles, hardships and distresses; in beatings, imprisonments and riots; in hard work, sleepless nights and hunger; in purity, understanding, patience and kindness; in the Holy Spirit and in sincere love; in truthful speech and in the power of God; with weapons of righteousness in the right hand and in the left; through glory and dishonor, bad report and good report; genuine, yet regarded as imposters; known, yet regarded as unknown; dying, and yet we live on; beaten, and yet not killed; sorrowful, yet always rejoicing; poor, yet making many rich; having nothing, and yet possessing everything" (2 Cor. 6:4–10).

Elsewhere Paul gives a very similar testimony about how he sees his life. "You, however, know all about my teaching, my way of life, my purpose, faith, patience, love, endurance, persecutions, sufferings—what kinds of things happened to me in Antioch, Iconium and Lystra, the persecutions I endured. Yet the Lord rescued me from all of them" (2 Tim. 3:10–11). It was in Antioch that Paul and Barnabas were persecuted and expelled from the city. In Iconium Jewish leaders joined with leading Gentiles to plot how they would stone Paul, but the plot was uncovered in time for Paul to flee from the city (see Acts 14:1–7). Lystra was the city where Paul was very nearly stoned to death by a mob that had been incited by some Jews coming in from Antioch and Iconium (see Acts 14:19–20). The apostle Paul was strengthened by the very experiences that were intended by his enemies to cause him to quit and to bring him to despair. No wonder Helen Keller, a spirited person like the apostle Paul, could say with conviction, "Character cannot be developed in ease and quiet. Only through experience of trial and suffering can the soul be strengthened, vision cleared, ambition inspired, and success achieved."

A few months ago our daughter, Sandy, was diagnosed with breast cancer. She asked for complete frankness from her oncologist, and he told her that the cancer was aggressive because the biopsy showed that it contained a resilient cancer cell that was difficult to destroy. He prescribed an aggressive treatment plan, which included eighteen weeks of chemotherapy, then two weeks of rest, then surgery, another two weeks of rest, and then thirty-three more weekly treatments. At the time of surgery, she would have to decide whether she would have the tumor surgically removed or would elect a mastectomy or a double mastectomy (to protect her health in the years to come).

After the first chemotherapy treatment, Sandy and Dave decided to do a four-day getaway with very close friends who had a beautiful condominium overlooking the ocean. After Sandy first rested for forty-eight hours following her chemotherapy, the family packed up and headed to the ocean. The first time everyone got ready to head to the ocean breakers, Sandy was so exhausted just changing into her beachwear that she encouraged her family to go enjoy the water while she rested. She would join them in an hour or so.

The weekend drive home from the beach took several hours and Sandy found it to be very taxing. Just three days later, on Wednesday morning, Joanne and I received a deeply concerned call from Dave at a hospital emergency room, asking us to come and pick up the girls as soon as we could. Sandy had been experiencing excruciating pain in her abdominal area and was rushed to the hospital in the middle of the night. Over a period of about five hours, the attending physician had given Sandy the maximum allowable dose of pain medication, yet the pain was still unbearable.

We had an hour-and-a-half drive to the Philadelphia area. I am one of those drivers who actually follows the speed limit (well, maybe a couple miles over), but under these urgent conditions I found myself driving ten miles over the posted limit. Joanne, who fears the consequence of high speeds even more than I do, turned to me and asked, "Bob, can't you go any faster?"

We arrived just two minutes before we were to pick up the girls at a neighbor's home. Charis and Syd, still in their pajamas, walked up the street with us to their house. Joanne headed to the hospital and I watched the girls, who were begging for sleep. During the next forty-eight hours, our family went through a cyclone-like series of events which included four major family consultations with medical and surgical staff, an emergency surgery to remove a section of incredibly diseased (but non-cancerous) intestine, and one by one, the activation of eight intravenous tubes that would simultaneously fight for her life drop by exactingly-measured drop.

Ten to fifteen family members and dear friends were with us in the waiting room at all times. Caring friends offered to be with Dave throughout the long night. I could not sleep at all at Dave and Sandy's home, so I went back to the hospital to see my daughter and spend some time with Dave. Sandy was totally immobile—even her eyelashes and fingers were still. Despite my efforts at some level of communication or conversation, there was absolutely no response or movement. I felt a sense of helplessness crawling inside me. If there was any semblance of calm in my demeanor, it was only because there were well over a hundred sincere family members and friends praying for Sandy, Dave, and our entire family.

The second day of hospitalization in the intensive care unit was even worse. Sandy's white cell count plummeted so low that it was a negligible factor in any possible recovery. Her heart had stopped and they promptly "coded" her, getting her heart beating again after a five-minute battle by several compassionate staff members. Sandy's kidneys had ceased to function—apparently shocked by the sheer overload of her many bodily needs. Her breathing was still totally dependent upon an artificial apparatus that gasped loudly in the quiet room, the closure valve even more audible, and at precisely timed intervals. About a dozen high tech monitors surrounded her, patiently and effortlessly taking countless readings.

Sometime during the endless second day of hospitalization, our family was called into a conference with compassionate but solemn staff who told us they had run out of options. We listened to their unenthused proposal for yet another surgery in her abdominal area. Dave said that he did not want Sandy to suffer any further—sobbing deeply as he spoke. We asked for thirty minutes as a family, then met with the medical staff to understand what pain Sandy might have to endure if we were to "let her go."

During the entire ordeal, we had four pastors visiting and encouraging us, as well as innumerable family members and friends who gave the impression that time now meant nothing to them. It was as though these dear friends had all the time in the world. No one hurried away to do other pressing matters. We were never alone. That was incredibly comforting.

Around midnight, about a dozen of us formed a circle around Sandy's hospital bed. Medical staff, given the agonizing consent of Dave as her husband and Joanne and I as her parents, would close down the artificial breathing apparatus which was only prolonging and extending a hopeless situation and giving the false impression that she was still alive and breathing. Her body gave no evidence at all of the shutdown. There was not the slightest tremor or gasp. Looking back, it seemed to me that she had been mercifully escorted from earth to heaven, likely at least twenty-four hours earlier, leaving behind the discarded and useless remnant of her absolutely lifeless body, albeit artificially oxygenated for some time.

We sang two of the great hymns of the church, had two short impromptu prayers consecrated with our tears. Unhurriedly, we left her silent, still body and re-gathered in the waiting room. Our waiting was now over. We now knew the outcome.

I felt numb. The fast-paced series of highly personal and significantly costly events had a surreal feeling for me. Not really understanding God's purpose, I still trusted him. I remember saying to friends, "I do not understand why God would take a mother away from her twin daughters when they are only eight years of age, but I do believe that God wills us no ultimate harm. It will take time for us to find our new roles as family members with Sandy now in heaven. But I believe that God is still with us moment by moment." I also remember saying something I learned in seminary some forty years earlier. "We are God's servants, he is not ours."

When we all headed down to the parking garage, I tried to lighten up for a moment. "Check back with me in about ten years and I will likely have a few answers! I am wonderful at hindsight!" Our car engines turned on energetically, but we dragged ourselves homeward with heavy hearts and relentless tears. Our entire world had suddenly turned gray.

Despite the suddenness and shock of the whole devastating experience, I was surprised again and again by the gracious presence of God. As a family we believe Christ's promise that, "In my Father's house are many rooms. . . . I am going there to prepare a place for you" (John 14:2). We were deeply touched when nearly three hundred persons gathered for Sandy's memorial service. Dave was enabled to give a beautiful and moving personal tribute to his wife at the very beginning of the worship service. It was five- or six-minutes long, and Dave said he was able to do it only because friends had prayed specifically for his strength and courage. Five close friends of Sandy (and Dave) gave their own inspiring testimonials about their friendship with Sandy.

There were other notable blessings. On the last day of Sandy's life, Dave's stepdad, sister, and brother came to the hospital to embrace and support Dave after several years of estrangement, bearing in their hearts an unconditional love and forgiveness. As a family, we also felt grateful that Sandy was mercifully spared the much larger pain, anguish, weakness, and uncertainty of a year-long program of aggressive chemotherapy.

Also, it would have been a far more brutal experience had this same scenario occurred after ten or eleven months of intensive chemotherapy. And I do not consider it lightly that the nurse who was assigned to Sandy on the last day of her earthly life shared her exact same date of birth.

Because Charis and Syd had lost both their mother and teacher (Sandy had homeschooled them for three years), our family had to make immediate decisions about their education. We inquired at the Valley Christian School in Huntingdon Valley in the Philadelphia area just three days before the fall semester began. The administrator, Susan Caler[7], arranged with her board not only to accept them without troubling us with all the paperwork so that our girls could be there for the first day of school, but also to reduce their tuition by $2,500. We all felt so grateful when the girls came running out of school that first critical day full of excitement about their teacher, "Miss Dougherty!"[8]

Because Sandy's death occurred so suddenly, it was difficult for Joanne and me to get hold of the reality of our loss. One of the things that helped me during that first week following her death was to find a quiet place where I could think about the significance of our daughter's life. It was for me one of the most meaningful ways of beginning the whole unwanted, life-altering process of grieving. It took me a few months to discover that God intends this largely negative experience (in terms of the way we usually see it) to be an important part of life. Because of God's continuing love for us in our pain and the Holy Spirit's reassurance of our loved one's resurrection, we have the possibility of further trusting God. We can continue our walk in Christ, proclaim God's goodness to the world, and express our gratitude to him for a particular relationship that was a significant source of joy over the course of many years. Writing this piece titled "Thanks, Lord, For the Gift of a Daughter" was for me a first step in trusting God and thanking him for the blessing Sandy was to us for more than forty years:

Thanks, Lord, For the Gift of a Daughter

Joanne tells me that the pregnancy test is positive.
The mystery of life is being nurtured inside my wife—
Tiny fingers and tiny toes forming in the darkness of her womb
She takes my hand gently one evening,
Placing it on the firm roundness of her swelling belly
I wait a few moments for what she wants me to know.
I hold my breath and listen.
And then . . . the soft bump of a tiny unseen foot kicking from within!
"He's going to be a soccer player," I say, grinning.
The moment comes when I hold you as our newborn daughter for the
        first time,
Feeling the threshold of life trembling in my hands.
You are the breathtaking gift of God!
The Creator is still creating.
Thanks, Lord, for the gift of a daughter!
Thanks for the magical years of childhood
And your marvelous and imaginative world of pretend.
I remember getting comfortable on the floor to color pictures with
        you.
And early on you carried your loveable "Patches" everywhere you
        went.
I enjoyed your tea parties on our sun porch when I came home for
        lunch.
I recall how you would improvise your own fun with our pots and
        pans
That made wonderful cymbal-like sounds when struck with spatulas.
In no time at all you were enjoying helping mom make a batch of
        cookies,
Licking the oversized spoon, wide-eyed.
Thanks, Lord, for the priceless gift of a daughter.
I treasure the memory of our lingering Saturday
        morning breakfasts
And evening snacks as a family while sharing personal stories and
        laughter;
Our walks late at night to get milk or treats at our corner store
Mom and I recall with delight how you danced around our living
        room,

Joyously celebrating your first crush with first-grader Kevin!
It lasted three full days.
Then you told us casually, "Kevin ran out of love."
We played family board games like Candyland and later Monopoly.
And I taught you that winning was secondary to us having fun.
I smile, remembering your well schemed "chimney scare" at dark
That made me jump a mile.
And how you jogged with me around the high school track at age five
And I loved it when you helped me rake the autumn leaves.
And in winter's deepest snow, we walked like robots to our corner
    store,
Making snow angels in the elegant drifts of a pristine winter
    wonderland—
Then marching back through our same deep footprints for hot
    chocolate with Mom
And of course screaming roller coaster rides at Great Adventure—
Often two or three times in succession
And building sandcastles with moats always needing more water,
And playing "Tank Game" and "Pac Man" with a mutual passion!
Thanks, Lord, for the special gift of a daughter.
For our sharing in the challenging journey from childhood to
    adulthood,
Encouraging you on the path to becoming a young woman.
It meant so much to you that I had picked out a special dress for you
Without Mom's coaching.
I loved meeting you for a spontaneous lunch out when you worked at
    the bank,
But found it a little less joyous reading your college essays after
    midnight,
In a state of numbness giving you requested feedback;
And likewise getting up around 3:00 A.M. to fix you a
    caffeinated snack
To help you survive your "all-nighter."
I know I did not send you fun letters frequently enough during your
    college days,
But I was thrilled when you told me that you had kept them all!
We had so much fun on our all-night drive from Florida to
    Pennsylvania—
A daddy-daughter adventure.

I was amazed at how you stayed awake and talked non-stop.
And Mom and I enjoyed honoring you in the spring before your
    wedding day
With our home surrounded solely with white flowers.
And I recall our coming to clean your apartment to de-stress the
    bride-to-be
When you were sick with a migraine just days before your wedding.
Thanks, Lord, for giving us a beautiful daughter,
To whom you gave a loving and patient husband (well, usually!)—
A man who gave his confusing life totally to your Son,
Seeking with all his heart to be all that you expected.
Sandy and Dave, you were both highly committed to honesty and
    purity—
The one trained in God's love through the years,
The other a prodigal who wandered far from home;
Yet both fully redeemed by the Savior's death,
Coming together in the oneness of marriage—
God's remarkable and joyous gift to you both.
You wrote your own vows for your wedding day.
They were beautiful and mature—and the longest I had ever seen!
I teased you: "Do you really want to commit this much?"
Both of you desired a solid Christian marriage.
Both of you truly loved one another.
Both of you gave everything you had within you.
Both of you believed that Christ was the Way to grow.
We admired the years when you both toughed it out
To achieve Dave's seminary degree and ordination into ministry.
We were inspired by the way you homeschooled Charis and Syd as a
    team,
Giving them a solid foundation of faith in Jesus.
Together you gave so much to pursue carefully God's will for your
    union
As man and wife,
But also as father and mother,
As son and daughter,
And as disciples of Christ the Lord.
Thanks, Lord, for the gift of a daughter,
Who shared with Dave the wonder of giving birth to twin girls,

A beautiful gift to them and a beautiful gift to us—
Transposing our lives into the joyous role of grandparents!
We took on the challenge of getting the baby food into their little
     mouths
Before their heads spun half circle to see who just walked in!
We enjoyed being a part of their bedtime prayers and nightly
     tuck-ins.
Joanne also enjoyed having new reasons for shopping—
Delighted to shop with Charis and Syd at Target
With the girls showing Grandmom where everything was!
And thanks, Sandy and Dave, for sharing special
     occasions with us—
Memories like "Disney on Ice®" and their first "Build-A-Bear®"
Mom and I enjoyed the many times you gently teased us
About the frequency of snacks and treats at our home—
Affectionately nicknamed "Sugar Land"
But most of all we respected your way of parenting.
Syd and Charis were always fairly disciplined by both you and Dave,
Your five-minute time-outs consistently given
You were loving and vigilant parents who never sat indifferently on
     the sofa.
When one or both were getting into trouble
Eyeball to eyeball you gently instructed them in godly behavior,
With large blocks of time for tickling them,
Or actively participating in their vivid pretend world,
Taking on the role of almost any assigned character;
And running backyard races around our four tallest trees;
And reading the classics to your girls as you drove back home.
Thanks, Lord, for the gift of a dear daughter,
Now set free of all suffering and pain—
Any and all fears now quieted by the fullness of your peace.
Thanks for escorting her home to be with you,
And with millions who have received the gifts of your forgiveness and
     grace.
Thanks so much, dear Lord, for lending her to us for a good long
     while.
Receive our gratitude for the hope of eternal life that we share in
     Christ.

Sandy, I will dance with you again as we did at your wedding,
And Mom and I will always remember the joy you were to us,
And still are to us, in memory, each day.
Thanks, Lord, for the gift of a daughter.

A Prayer

O Lord, how you suffered on the cross to atone for my sin and provide for my salvation! Help me to bear my own suffering and setbacks with courage and cheerfulness, that others may see in me the love of Christ empowering my life. Help me to understand that your will for my life ultimately is never harm, but is for my greater good. Grant that I might mature in my faith in you as I go through the tight spaces in my life. Through the graciousness of your Holy Spirit, flush from my heart all of my anger, resentment, and bad attitude toward my difficulties, and restore in me patience, perseverance, and an interest in others. As I pass through those experiences that are like deep waters or fire, sustain me with your strength and peace, so that I might testify to your love, thanking you at all times for your many generous blessings. I pray in the name of Jesus whose suffering on the cross has become a huge blessing to countless millions. Amen.

Three Questions

1. Do you see your sufferings and setbacks as unwanted interruptions to your life, and therefore resent them? Does a biblical understanding of suffering help us when we are locked into a negative view? How?

2. Do you see any difference between the way a mature Christian and an unbeliever processes their problems, disappointments, and setbacks? If so, explain why the responses could be different. If you see no difference, can you support your position?

3. Have you ever felt inspired as a result of knowing someone who suffered a major setback, yet remained an uncomplaining, loving, and grateful person? You might want to take time to describe the person's attitude and behavior and set of circumstances, and why he/she inspired you.

INSIGHTS

My mind is absorbed with the sufferings of man. Since I was twenty-four there never [has been] any vagueness in my plans or ideas as to what God's work was for me.

—Florence Nightingale

You will never find a better sparring partner than adversity.

—Walt Schmidt

We are not at our best perched at the summit; we are climbers, at our best when the way is steep.

—John W. Gardner

The chief pang of most trials is not so much the actual suffering itself as our own spirit of resistance to it.

—Jean Nicolas Grou

I do not believe that sheer suffering teaches. If suffering alone taught, then all the world would be wise, since everyone suffers. To suffering must be added mourning, understanding, patience, love, openness, and the willingness to remain vulnerable.

—Anne Morrow Lindbergh

A diamond is a chunk of coal that made good under pressure.

—Henry Kissinger

Suffering, although it is a burden, is a useful burden, like the splints used in orthopedic treatment.

—Soren Kierkegaard

The real problem is not why some pious, humble believing people suffer, but why some do not.

—C. S. Lewis

He who fears to suffer cannot be His who suffered.

—Tertullian

CHAPTER TEN

Do not think that because you are in the king's house you alone of all the Jews will escape. For if you remain silent at this time, relief and deliverance for the Jews will arise from another place, but you and your father's family will perish. And who knows but that you have come to royal position for such a time as this?
—Est. 4:12–14

$\mathcal{J}$HEDDING $\mathcal{J}$ELFI$\mathcal{J}$HNE$\mathcal{J}$

INTERPERSONAL

After serving troubled congregations for thirty-five years, and dealing with Parkinsons for two years while fully employed, Joanne and I decided to retire two years earlier than planned because of my health problems. After serving small churches all my life, we decided to be a part of Derry Presbyterian Church in Hershey, Pennsylvania—an active 1,100 member missional church with strong pastoral leadership. I felt burned out and needed a place to regroup. Derry became our retreat center. It was wonderful to sit with my wife, share a hymnbook, hold hands during the prayers, and be spiritually refreshed by the inspirational messages ably preached by the Rev. Dick Houtz and the Rev. Marie Buffaloe—sermons I did not have to write!

During our first year at Derry we met Henry Nixon,[9] one of Derry's members who had supported many mission trips throughout his life. When he was in elementary school he enthusiastically saved his pennies to buy bricks for a mission project in Chile. As he approached his ninetieth birthday, he attended a church presentation by one of the church's mission teams who had just returned from Nicaraugua as volunteers who built modest homes for the poor. He realized that there was no way that he could do the strenuous work.

The volunteers mixed their own concrete on the bare ground. They also manually wired together bars of reinforcing steel to make each concrete block home able to withstand hurricanes.

Henry wanted to be a part of their ongoing mission project so he celebrated his ninetieth birthday by donating $2,500 to cover the cost of all the materials needed to construct a modest concrete block home in Nicaraugua. Each year since, Henry has given significant support to this annual week-long mission project of building homes for families previously living in rusty, corrugated sheet metal shacks. This ministry has built over twenty-five homes, our own volunteers working alongside native Nicarauguans. Henry is now ninety-seven years old!

Back when Henry was ninety, Joanne and I had just purchased our retirement home and were thrilled to be homeowners once again. Following Henry's example, Joanne and I decided to find a way to sponsor one of the two homes that were to be built in the summer of 2004, as a thank offering to God for the beautiful retirement home that we had recently purchased. Since then we have donated six homes, one as a Christmas project of our family, one as a Bible study group commitment, and several others over the years by teaming up with another couple, Tom and Nancy Kitzmiller[10], who share our vision.

The homes that we have helped to build are very modest in size—approximately the size of a generous family room in one of today's suburban homes. They have one door, one window, no interior dividing walls, and the interior space measures about fifteen by twenty-five feet. The recipient family typically has two or three children. One mother said to a few of our team members, "I was so thankful that the rain no longer splashed on my children's faces as they slept."

INSPIRING

> Then Esther summoned Hathach, one of the king's eunuchs assigned to attend her, and ordered him to find out what was troubling Mordecai and why. So Hathach went out to Mordecai in the open square of the city in front of the king's gate. Mordecai told him everything that had happened to him, including the exact amount of money Haman had promised to pay into the

royal treasury for the destruction of the Jews. He also gave him a copy of the text of the edict for their annihilation, which had been published in Susa, to show to Esther and explain it to her, and he told him to urge her to go into the king's presence to beg for mercy and plead with him for her people. Hathach went back and reported to Esther what Mordecai had said. Then she instructed him to say to Mordecai, "All the king's officials and the people of the royal provinces know that for any man or woman who approaches the king in the inner court without being summoned the king has but one law: that he be put to death. The only exception to this is for the king to extend the gold scepter to him and spare his life. But thirty days have passed since I was called to go to the king." When Esther's words were reported to Mordecai, he sent back this answer: "Do you think that because you are in the king's house you alone of all the Jews will escape? For if you remain silent at this time, relief and deliverance for the Jews will arise from another place, but you and your father's family will perish. And who knows but that you have come to royal position for such a time as this?" Then Esther sent this reply to Mordecai: "Go, gather together all the Jews who are in Susa, and fast for me. Do not eat or drink for three days, night or day. I and my maids will fast as you do. When this is done, I will go to the king, even though it is against the law. And if I perish, I perish."

—Est. 4:5–16

IMAGING

Queen Esther, What Will You Do?

Esther, adopted child of your uncle Mordecai
Loved by him as a daughter,
You are caught in a dangerous situation.
What will you do?
These are not happy days like those when you won Persia's beauty
    pageant,
Winning the great honor of being the nation's queen,
Thereafter reigning in the splendor of the elegant palace in Susa,
Where wine is served in goblets of gold.
Ever since your uncle learned of Haman's sinister plot to exterminate
    every Jew in Persia,

You have felt anxious, confused, and fearful.
And when Mordecai briefed you about Haman's edict of intended
    atrocities,
You wondered what your role could possibly be in this dangerous
    game.
So you discussed it with your most trusted maids and eunuchs:
"I am not sure that I can be even a small part of the solution to this
    problem,
But, if so, what would you advise me to do?"
"My queen, you are so lovely and so sweet to all," one maid began.
"And you are young and have your whole life before you!
Do not spoil all that by getting involved in this political mess.
You could be swept away in the violence."
But you know you cannot remain silent,
Especially when learning that Haman has offered a colossal amount
    of silver to your king
To gain his permission to eliminate the Jews as a so-called menace to
    the state.
Haman is passionately committed to his gruesome business,
And you are not willing to simply save your neck.
Oh, Queen Esther, whose beauty still captivates tens of thousands,
What will you do?
Another maid stepped forward to advise.
"Dearest Queen Esther, I fully agree. This is something that you do
    not need to be involved in.
Haman has vast powers to execute his orders,
Powers given to him by your king,
Powers that can never be revoked.
You're just one person after all,
And one person cannot possibly make any difference."
You listen with a heavy heart, and then glance down at the edict
Unrolled on the table beside you.
It is true!
Haman plans to exterminate your race,
Including every woman and child!
There has to be something you can do as queen.
Surely, you have power too!
Then one of your most trusted eunuchs stood to offer his wisdom.

"My queen, you are the most charming and most beautiful woman in
    Persia.
I urge you to be cautious.
We can provide you security as long as you stay here in this fortress.
There are so many things you could do for our nation
Once we get beyond this peril—
Like teaching our women to appreciate and enhance their unique
    beauty
Not merely outwardly,
But encouraging them to strive to be beautiful from within,
As you are.
You could teach countless thousands how to be gracious, loving, and
    kind,
How to do deeds of goodness and mercy that could affect our whole
    culture,
And so make our nation stronger, and our marriages and families
    happier.
Everyone respects you and holds you in honor.
I counsel you not to do anything
That could send the wrong message to your people,
Or possibly diminish your great reputation."
But, Esther, you can only think of the danger that is already inside
    your palace.
And if you approach your king in the inner court without being
    summoned,
Even you could be instantly put to death.
Besides, how could you help your people to become happier if
    Haman's plan succeeds?
Is not this the hour to be courageous, not cautious?
But all of your indecision dissolves when you receive a second
    message from your uncle,
A gentle man who was like a loving father to you.
His message is forceful and scolding, so unlike him you thought.
"Do you think that you alone of all the Jews will escape?
If you do not stand up to Haman, even your life will perish.
And who knows!
Perhaps you have been placed on the throne for such a time as this."
His message shook you out of your ambivalence, giving you a great
    resolve.

185

You called for your secretary and gave your uncle your reply at once.
"Uncle Mordecai, gather all the Jews and fast for me.
My maids and I will do the same.
Once we have done this I will approach the king on the matter and
    expose Haman.
And should I perish, I perish."
O Esther, inspiring queen of a great nation,
You have found your task in a dangerous time.
You have spared us a holocaust for a few more millennia.
May we, like you, discover our role in a complex and frequently
    dangerous world.
And may we, like you, have the courage to act and take our stand,
Even when the price could be a precious life like yours.

INTERPRETING

When Esther sends her final response to her uncle Mordecai, she
underscores how costly his request could be. "I will go to the king,
even though it is against the law. And if I perish, I perish" (Est. 4:16).
Did she want to be sure that her uncle understood that he was asking
her to put her life on the line? Did he understand that she was out of
touch with her king and more than one uninvited intruder had been
instantly put to death by the palace guards?

Her response gives us some insight into her feelings and clearly
tells us that she had considerable difficulty doing what her uncle
so emphatically challenged her to do. Risking your life for the sake
of others is the ultimate act of selflessness. Jesus taught us this lofty
principle when he said, "Greater love has no one than this, that he lay
down his life for his friends" (John 15:13).

Was Esther courageous? Or was she trembling with fear? Both
seem to be true. Years ago, while waiting my turn in a small barber-
shop, I had a conversation with a man who had served as a para-
trooper in Korea. After thanking him for his service to our country
by performing highly dangerous missions, our conversation turned
to the subject of courage. "You must possess a great deal of courage
to do as many jumps as you have done," I remarked. "Well, I really
do not have a lot of courage," he replied. "I guess it depends on how
you understand courage. I have the same anxiety and fears that you

or anyone else might have. But, to me, courage is throwing yourself out of the plane along with your fears."

Queen Esther would have fully understood what he was saying. She could not rid herself of the possibility that something might be wrong between Xerxes and herself. Why else had he failed to call for her to have an evening together? Moreover, Xerxes' personal body-guards were well known for their swiftness. She might never make it across the imperial room to touch the king's scepter. Yet Esther decided to take that risk despite the nauseous feeling in her stomach and the fears that were stirring up doubts in her heart.

Doing the selfless and loving act does not always give us a good feeling. There are occasions when we experience an inner peace or joy, or the fulfillment that comes on the heels of helping someone through a crisis. At such times we have that satisfying feeling inside which says, *This is what I was created to do!* But there may be other times when the selfless act puts you in danger, or makes you vulnerable, or financially requires sacrifice. Couples who decide to adopt a child living in an orphanage in Russia or China may spend twenty or thirty thousand dollars before successfully bringing the child to the States, and in addition also endure considerable anxiety as they run the gauntlet of countless forms to process, distrust from authorities, political unrest, unexpected changes in requirements, and months of waiting. We remember Esther because of her selflessness and love for her people.

Esther was not only courageous. She was also humble. Most likely this quality was taught her by her uncle, Mordecai. Too many of us do not follow the instincts, counsel, or wisdom of those who are twenty to thirty years older. Esther likely had a great respect for her uncle and carefully considered what he had to say. Throughout her childhood, had she sat on her uncle's lap talking with him, and so had come to love and respect him? As a young girl, did she want to be like him in terms of his love, gentleness, kindness, and integrity? Mordecai is likely the one who should be most credited for Esther's courage, self-esteem, graciousness, humility, compassion, selflessness, and inner beauty.

Quite often the selfless act that we are contemplating has an uncertain outcome and consequently involves some risk. To illustrate, let us suppose that you share a friendship with another couple (at your church) who again and again show disrespect for one another, causing you to be concerned for them. After a season of prayer for them, you might decide that the husbands should get together over lunch and sensitively discuss it. The outcome might be wonderful, or it could be disastrous! You could be seen as intrusive or even smug. If your intentions are misunderstood, your efforts to reach out could hurt your friendship indefinitely. Are you willing to assume that risk in the hope of lovingly strengthening their marriage? Can you go about it with a sense of humility rather than coming across as haughty or condescending? Would you begin with personal stories about your own times of showing disrespect to your mate when you were yet unaware of its hurtful impact?

If you were to meet with a friend to share some insights that could enrich their marriage, you need to reassure them that you are a fellow struggler. And you need to feel equally comfortable learning from your friend's observations about *your* marriage. Acting selflessly on behalf of another is not as easy as it looks. The selfless act needs to be guided and tempered by a genuine humility, the preparation of prayer, graciousness, restraint, sensitivity, and love.

INTEGRATING

I was raised in Baltimore where the Juvenile Court of the State of Maryland is located. As you enter that court there is a compelling statement obviously placed there to get juvenile offenders to re-think the purpose for their lives. It says:

> Happiness is not having what you want, but wanting
>   what you have.
> Life is an exciting business, and most exciting when
>   lived for others.

The basic thrust of that statement originates with Jesus, who put it even more simply: "As I have loved you, so you must love one another" (John 13:34). This was one of his closing teachings at the last supper in the upper room, when he emphasized it more than once: "My command is this: Love each other as I have loved you. Greater love has no one than this, that he lay down his life for his friends" (John 15:12–13). Jesus' statement causes us immediately to think of his sacrificial death on the cross, which of course was his redemptive mission for the sake of the world. But in terms of *our* mission, it is more likely that Jesus is referring to day-by-day acts of self-giving, gestures of love, and thoughtful kindnesses, such as preparing a meal for someone coming home from the hospital or cleaning out an elderly person's basement as he prepares to sell his house and move into his daughter's home.

Excepting prayer, I cannot think of any other characteristic that has such power to reshape our marriages as this quality of selflessness. Selflessness rises at daybreak to good-humoredly get the children up and dressed and then hustles to the kitchen to begin pulling things together for breakfast, not because of some burdensome sense of duty, but because of the vitality that the Holy Spirit generates in our hearts, enabling us to express the love of Christ. In his selfless love, you grab a pad and jot down, "Matt, I hope you ace your history test today. You know what works best for you—taking a deep breath and settling into the work of recalling the highlights. I will be praying for you. Dad."

At the workplace his selfless love abiding in you enables you to warmly congratulate Ned as the honored employee of the month. But you are soon aware of a gray hint of jealousy making its play for your heart. To rid yourself of that feeling, you decide to invite Ned to lunch. On your drive home after work, you're feeling tired. Nevertheless, you still find joy in cutting some slack to a frustrated driver trapped on a smaller side street, both of you locked in by bumper-to-bumper work traffic.

Back home, you quickly wrestle your coat off and check to see whether it would be better to help your wife get supper underway or shoot some baskets with Neal and find out how things went at prac- tice. Throughout the evening, the selfless love of Christ empowers you from within, enabling you to be focused on family members, knowing

189

that if anyone has had a tough day, signs of it will likely show on their face or in their slumped posture. When the selflessness of Christ is our course, God's love is at full tilt. Is that the way it is for you?

Finding the Energy to Keep Giving Selflessly

Let me be candid. The person I just described is definitely not me. I have had Parkinsons for over ten years, and my greatest problem is endurance. I have learned how to pace myself. I still enjoy volunteering with Lend A Hand to help rebuild hurricane-ravaged homes hundreds of miles from our town. However, each time I sign up, Joanne is genuinely concerned about how I will hold up. *I am concerned about how I will hold up!* I ask my family and friends to pray for me, and they do. When the week is over and I reflect on it, it is usually always the same. My work performance was probably the lowest on the team of twenty to thirty volunteers. I am unbeatable when it comes to rest breaks, both in number and duration!

Nevertheless, God uses our gifts despite our weakness. I may be just sitting on a stump trying to revive with a cup of coffee while chatting with a discouraged homeowner from down the road. Rebuilding after a disaster requires more than simply nailing studs into place. Our mission is twofold. We are gutting and rebuilding houses that were almost carried away by floodwaters. We are also rebuilding hope in the hearts of those who have lost nearly everything and who are immobilized by the shock of a catastrophe like nothing they have ever seen.

When Paul writes to the church in Corinth, he shares with them how he suffers from a thorn in his flesh (see 2 Cor. 12:7). Some scholars believe he may have been suffering from painful arthritis and had repeatedly pleaded with God to "take it away from me" (12:8). The answer he received was nothing like what he requested: "My grace is sufficient for you, for my power is made perfect in weakness" (2 Cor. 12:9).

That's where we can confidently step into this—on the word *weakness*! Have you ever wondered how a medical missionary in Ghana can do fifteen to twenty cataract surgeries each day in a totally inadequate tent hospital? Have you ever been awed by Christian authors who write fifteen or twenty books that are inspiring, creative, thought-provoking, and totally faithful to Scripture? There seems to be only one explanation. They do not do it with their own strength. They depend on the power of God.

The Scriptures make it incredibly simple. I personally conclude that such enthusiastic, energetic, and enjoyable persons are constantly empowered by the Holy Spirit. The apostle Paul admits, "We are weak in him [Christ], *yet by God's power* we will live with him to serve . . . " (2 Cor. 13:4, emphasis mine). Our inheritance as members of the body of Christ includes not only the precious life-giving words of Christ, but also the power of the Holy Spirit that energizes our bodies to physically do the workings of his will.

Consequently, Paul offers an amazing insight into how God works in us when he says to the young Christians in Thessalonica, "For we know, brothers loved by God, that he has chosen you, because our gospel came to you *not simply with words, but also with power*, with the Holy Spirit and with deep conviction" (1 Thess. 1:4–5, emphasis mine). Paul is not simply talking about a *spiritual* power that strengthens our faith with conviction, although the Holy Spirit does that also.

When he writes to the Colossians, Paul is urging them to bear fruit and to "live a life worthy of the Lord" (Col. 1:10). In no way does he imply that they are just going to have to tough it out and learn how to pace themselves while doing all of the worthy things that take time and energy but also give glory to God. Instead, he commands my attention as a Parkinsons patient by talking about how God pumps up our endurance as we go about loving our neighbor and doing good. "And we pray . . . that you may live a life worthy of the Lord and may please him in every way: *bearing fruit in every good work*, growing in the knowledge of God, *being strengthened with all power according to his glorious might so that you may have great endurance and patience*" (Col. 1:10–11, emphasis mine).

Dare we believe this is so? The next time God nudges you to be a role model and coordinator for middle school youth, can you say yes without wondering whether you will have the endurance needed to keep up with young, high-energy teens? Or can you tell the Lord that you would love to honor his call, but you will definitely need to be strengthened day-by-day with a generous serving of "his glorious might" into your body and spirit?

This is an area in which I need to demonstrate greater faith. As a husband and as a believer, I spend too much precious time assessing whether I have the time (or strength) to do the things that bring joy to my wife—whether we are talking about preparing beef burgundy for a special dinner for two, or cutting down a diseased tree that has become a noticeable eyesore on the front of our property. Is it possible that our faith in Christ is calling us to less assessment of our calendar and less evaluation of our strength, so that we can make our decisions in the full knowledge that we really have very little strength in and of ourselves, but have the vast power of God freely offered to us at all times? And consequently, "I can do everything through him who gives me strength" (Phil. 4:13).

Is it possible that some of us live as we do, cautious about making new commitments and virtually blindsided to God's tremendous resources freely available to us through "his glorious might"? Perhaps it is easier, or feels more safe and secure, to say that such and such a commitment could put my health at risk.

A Prayer

Astonishing Lord, you have made life an adventure by giving me the freedom to make choices in life that demonstrate my courage and love and my trust in your guiding hand. And by my own self-centeredness, I have narrowed the fullness of life you wanted for me down to a little world primarily wrapped up in myself— a world which inevitably becomes boring due to its smallness. Dear Lord, who has given us a breathtaking world splashed with a thousand different colors and hues, open my eyes to the innumerable possibilities for my life that would enrich the lives of others while simultaneously increasing my own joy and deepening my faith in you. What risk you have taken in giving to me and millions of others the power to choose how each day will be spent! I pray that today and tomorrow I will by faith more gladly pursue your will, knowing that whatever challenging task you call me to, you also will generously enable me to do it through your glorious might empowering me in body and spirit. In Christ my Lord I pray. Amen.

Three Questions

1. Think about the different personalities in your church fellowship. Are there persons who come to mind who seem not only to get the Lord's work done, but at the same time are tireless and joyous in doing it?

2. Why do you suppose that some Christians seem to have so little vitality, so little excitement for their faith?

3. Looking back over your life, what commitment or experience do you remember that caused you to stretch and grow, but at the same time frightened you (or at least intimidated you) in terms of a looming doubt about your capacity to do it, even knowing that it was something that would please God?

INSIGHTS

The entire law is summed up in a single command: "Love your neighbor as yourself."

—Gal. 5:14

You can always tell when a man is a great way from God: when he is always talking about himself, how good he is.

—Dwight L. Moody

If anyone would come after me, he must deny himself and take up his cross and follow me.

—Matt. 16:24

The first lesson in Christ's school is self-denial.

—Matthew Henry

He who falls in love with himself will have no rivals.

—Benjamin Franklin

The entire population of the universe, with one trifling exception, is composed of others.

—John Andrew Holmes

A man wrapped up in himself makes a very small package.

—Benjamin Franklin

Men are not against you; they are merely for themselves.

—Gene Fowler

God defend me from myself.

—Michel de Montaigne

God sends no one away empty except those who are full of themselves.

—Dwight L. Moody

It is not the self that must be destroyed, but the Satanic spirit of egotism in the self.

—Norman P. Grubb

We are rich only through what we give, and poor only through what we refuse.

—Anne-Sophie Swetchine

CHAPTER ELEVEN

Do nothing out of selfish ambition or vain conceit, but in humility consider others better than yourselves. Each of you should look not only to your own interests, but also to the interests of others. Your attitude should be the same as that of Christ Jesus: Who, being in very nature God, did not consider equality with God something to be grasped, but made himself nothing, taking the very nature of a servant, being made in human likeness.

—Phil. 2:3–7

CONSIDERING OTHERS AS BETTER—HUMILITY

INTERPERSONAL

J oanne and I were excited about the prospect of experiencing small town life, since both of us had lived in large cities all our lives. I was to preach as a candidate at the Penningtonville Presbyterian Church in Atglen, Pennsylvania, a small town with just one traffic signal. As we approached this simple country church with its modest steeple, it seemed as though one of the Currier and Ives greeting cards had come to life!

We enjoyed the down-to-earth greetings and strong handshakes, the warm welcome offered during worship, and the singing of familiar hymns. After I had preached and our worship was concluded, Joanne and I were excused so that the congregation could discuss whether they would extend an invitation to me to be their pastor. We waited longer than we had ever waited in any previous call process.

Finally, the moderator entered the room smiling. He told us the church had voted unanimously to call me. As Joanne and I climbed the stairs to the sanctuary, I asked the moderator what I thought was a routine question: "Would you tell me what the original vote was before it was made a unanimous call?" He stopped on the stairwell and said candidly, "Fifty-three in favor and twenty-one no's." Nearly a third of the active congregation did not favor my coming. I turned to

197

my wife, looking for an explanation for what amounted to a significant minority vote opposed to our coming. What had happened? I
asked the moderator if I could address the congregation briefly.

As I walked to the mike, I asked God to give me words that were
gracious and sensitive. I explained to the congregation that I had
chosen to serve troubled churches most of my life, and I was not
willing to risk creating such a problem in Atglen. I then concluded
by saying, "If I accepted this call, knowing the original voting results,
I would be creating a very poor start for both of us. I respect each
of your decisions, but at this moment, I have no understanding as
to what may have caused so many no votes. If you would care to
offer any light on that as we greet one another at the door, I would
be grateful. And I assure you that I will simply listen and not debate
your position or concerns."

One member offered this at the door: "I was one of the no's. The
reason I voted no was because I felt I had not been given adequate
information from our pastoral nominating committee about who you
are. But I was impressed by the sensitive way you explained to us your
decision not to take the call. If I were to vote right now I would be a yes."

Concerned elders, deacons, and members of the pastoral nominating
committee offered to stay as long as we had questions or concerns in
the hope of understanding why the day had unfolded as it did. We
concluded our time together at the home of one of the deacons.

What we discovered was a surprise to all of us. I was serving
a church that was only fifty miles away. The pastoral nominating
committee in Atglen was trying to protect the confidentiality of the
call to avoid any problems with my church in Roslyn, Pennsylvania,
should word somehow come to them that I was considering a new
call. In the process, the congregation received too little information
about my education, service, experience, and pastoral record.

After a barrage of concerned calls back and forth over the next
few days, the pastoral nominating committee provided everyone in
the church a copy of my entire dossier and gave the congregation the
opportunity to vote again. We gladly accepted the enthusiastic vote
and enjoyed eight eventful years of service with a highly committed
and wonderfully diverse people of God.

Inspiring

In the sixth month, God sent the angel Gabriel to Nazareth, a town in Galilee, to a virgin pledged to be married to a man named Joseph, a descendant of David. The virgin's name was Mary. The angel went to her and said, "Greetings, you who are highly favored! The Lord is with you."

Mary was greatly troubled at his words and wondered what type of greeting this might be. But the angel said to her, "Do not be afraid, Mary, you have found favor with God. You will be with child and give birth to a son, and you are to give him the name Jesus. He will be great and will be called the Son of the Most High. The Lord God will give him the throne of his father David, and he will reign over the house of Jacob forever; his kingdom will never end."

"How will this be," Mary asked the angel, "since I am a virgin?"

The angel answered, "The Holy Spirit will come upon you, and the power of the Most High will overshadow you. So the holy one to be born will be called the Son of God. Even Elizabeth your relative is going to have a child in her old age, and she who is said to be barren is in her sixth month. For nothing is impossible with God."

"I am the lord's servant," Mary answered. "May it be to me as you have said." Then the angel left her.

—Luke 1:26–38

Imagining

How Do You Go About Redeeming a World?

God formed ten thousand galaxies, but they are just the
    background—
The background for an event so amazing
No one could have come up with the idea
Except God!
When the news of God's glorious plan to redeem the world

Was first shared in the heavenlies,
It spread like wildfire,
Causing excited discussion everywhere,
Amazing the angels.
The Word was that God would send an angel to a small town girl
    named Mary,
Telling her that she would give birth to the Son of God!
The Eternal One would be miniaturized to fit inside
    a woman's womb.
The One with no beginning would mysteriously be formed inside
    Mary,
And she would give him the name Jesus.
He would be born in a Bethlehem barn,
And his kingdom would never end.

In one heavenly court ten thousand angels assembled
Because the news caused consternation and concern.
The presiding angel seemed visibly shaken by the news.
When he began his address to the assembly, you could have heard a
    pin drop.
His questions were those of one genuinely perplexed:
"Why would God choose this?" the angel began.
"Why would God *do* this?"
The angel boldly stated his concerns.
"I do not mean to sound arrogant before our most loving God,
But can this plan possibly work?
The girl selected is likely fourteen, fifteen at most,
So our glorious God will be trusting a young teen to carry
    the infinite One!
And Joseph will never comprehend Gabriel's message for his Mary,
Especially Gabriel's explanation about how she would be
Overshadowed by the Spirit of God.
So *why* on earth is our dear Lord choosing this lowly way?
My personal concern is that it has no sophistication, no attractiveness,
Nothing to command people's attention and respect.
Nazareth is much too small a town to attract any notice.
Besides, carrying the Son of God will put too much stress and strain
    on young Mary."
He paused for a few moments, trying to regain calm.

His next words were moving.
"Such a momentous event deserves the crash of cymbals,
The thunderous roll of drums,
The joyous melodies of many stringed instruments,
And the splendor of a royal court presiding with a hundred trumpets
    sounding.
God's Son deserves a noble escort of at least a thousand horsemen
With the glint of gold reflected off their saddles' trappings.
The presentation would be stronger with a monarch's title,
A king or emperor or sheik of immense power and wealth.
The choice of a small-town carpenter simply will not carry it!
Perhaps we need to petition our blessed Lord,
    full of glory and honor,
Asking *why* he would choose this mode of revelation.
Glorious angels of this vast region,
I have given the matter careful thought
And I doubt that it can be made to work,
    even by our majestic God.
Can the One who is to be the Light of the World
Form in the confined darkness of a young woman's womb
And then be born in a barn—
The only visitors, some common shepherds working the night shift,
And foreign kings coming too late and from too far to matter to
    anyone?
Angelic hosts, I fear that the whole plan will be seen as much too
    plain,
Too basic,
And too dull
To excite anyone."

The petition was written with every angel's concerns expressed.
God listened, considered,
And then responded respectfully and lovingly.
"Angelic hosts, thanks for your honest reflections and thoughtful
    concerns.
Yes, Nazareth is a small town, but small towns are filled with my
    people.
I will still send my angel Gabriel there to make my announcement.
Yes, Mary is a young teen,

But I cherish the way she trusts me.
I love her obedient nature and humility.
So she will give birth to my beloved Son and name him Jesus.
Yes, Joseph will find it most perplexing
To be told that Mary became pregnant by the power of the Most
    High;
But I will patiently help him understand.
And yes, hillside shepherds in their work clothes
Will be the only visitors that first week after my Son's birth;
But I will trust them to spread the excitement and joy of my Son's
    coming.
No, my Son will not be born of royalty,
Yet he will become King of all kings,
The Savior of the world!
This remains my plan
Because it expresses perfectly
The love and humility
That originate in me."

INTERPRETING

You seldom hear anyone refer to the humility of God. We speak of Jesus as "the servant of all" (Mark 9:35), but rarely speak of the humility of Jesus. Yet no one has ever walked this earth bearing in his or her life and character such fullness of humility as we find in Jesus Christ. We see it in the humble way he chose to come to us from the Father, as a vulnerable baby born to Mary in a barn in Bethlehem—a first century village that is known to millions across the world only because it is Jesus' birthplace. Mary "gave birth to her firstborn, a son. She wrapped him in cloths and placed him in a manger, because there was no room for them in the inn" (Luke 2:7). Behind the birth of Jesus we see the humility of God.

We also see it in the way God has provided for our redemption through Jesus' death on the cross. The first century Roman conquerors believed that the crucifixion of criminals was the strongest deterrent to crime. Crosses normally lined the highways so the people could witness the victims' excruciating pain and labored breathing. Yet that was what God the Father accepted for his beloved Son as the atonement, or payment, for the sin of the world.

The apostle Paul, trying to teach the Christians at Philippi to live humbly, saw a tie between Jesus' humility and our own humility as his followers. "Your attitude should be the same as that of Christ Jesus: Who, being in very nature God, did not consider equality with God something to be grasped, but made himself nothing, taking the very nature of a servant, being made in human likeness" (Phil. 2:5–7). Behind the death of Jesus, we see the humility of God.

Humility is also a recurring theme in Jesus' teachings. He once brought a child forward to stand before a crowd as a living illustration of humility. Then he said to the people, "I tell you the truth, unless you change and become like little children, you will never enter the kingdom of heaven. Therefore, whoever humbles himself like this child is the greatest in the kingdom of heaven" (Matt. 18:2–4). Luke recalls a similar situation in which Jesus has a little child stand beside him and then explains to his disciples, "Whoever welcomes this little child in my name welcomes me. For he who is least among you all—he is the greatest" (Luke 9:48).

More than once Jesus identifies greatness with service, a practice requiring humility. "The greatest among you will be your servant. For whoever exalts himself will be humbled, and whoever humbles himself will be exalted" (Matt. 23:11–12). Jesus totally identifies himself with the lowliest of humanity—the hungry, the homeless, the estranged, the imprisoned. He surprises us by turning upside down the human clamor for recognition, prestige, wealth, comfort, and achievement, and commended in its place the care of the poorest. "I tell you the truth, whatever you did for one of the least of these brothers of mine, you did for me" (Matt. 25:40). In Jesus' teachings, we learn about humility and service.

Moreover, Jesus is his own best illustration of his teachings on humility. Consider some of the commitments and experiences in his life and how they demonstrate his humility. An unknown author once said that Jesus "never owned a home." Our Lord never became distracted from his ministry by the desire to build a house for his own comfort and enjoyment. "Foxes have holes," he said, "and birds of the air have nests, but the Son of Man has no place to lay his head" (Matt. 8:20). When John the Baptist was preparing the people for Jesus' coming, John urged them to repent of their sins and be baptized in the Jordan as a sign of their new beginning. Jesus did not need to be baptized because he had never sinned; yet he is humble enough to come to John to be baptized. Matthew notes in his gospel how uneasy John the Baptist felt about baptizing Jesus. "But John tried to deter him, saying, 'I need to be baptized by you, and do you come to me?'" (Matt. 3:14).

Again and again you see Jesus' humility in his life experiences. When Jesus met with his disciples the evening before his crucifixion, he washed their feet. The way in which the gospel writer John introduces this graphic illustration of servanthood is striking: "*Jesus knew that the Father had put all things under his power, and that he had come from God and was returning to God;* so he got up from the meal, took off his outer clothing, and wrapped a towel around his waist. After that, he poured water into a basin and began to wash his disciples' feet, drying them with the towel that was wrapped around him" (John 13:3–5, emphasis mine). Even as Jesus taught his disciples humility with the unforgettable images of a basin and towel, he was fully aware of his own eternal nature, his life on earth being both preceded by, and followed by, his everlasting life with the Father. Humility is a constant in Jesus' life. Never does he step away from this spiritual trait.

And after Jesus vacates his grave, he meets his disciples on a familiar beach, where they haul in their boats after a discouraging night of fishing. Rather than seeing himself as a celebrity or wonder worker to be partied and applauded, Jesus chooses to build a charcoal fire and cook a hearty breakfast for these hungry, discouraged men. What an inspiring humility! Resurrected from his grave, he is the news story of the week, yet he spends hours serving and strengthening his disciples, standing with them as friend, and helping them to regroup. "Each of you should look not only to your own interests, but also to the interests of others" (Phil. 2:4). Jesus lived by that principle throughout his entire earthly life. We see in Jesus' life the astounding humility of God!

God's uniform, consistent nature confirms his divine humility. "Jesus Christ is the same yesterday and today and forever" (Heb. 13:8). Because Jesus is one with the Father, this statement from Hebrews about Jesus is equally true of God the Father. Whether we are looking at Jesus' birth in Bethlehem, his death by crucifixion, his hallmark teachings on being childlike and servant-like, or his day-by-day activities—washing his disciples' feet on one occasion and cooking them breakfast on another—we become aware of God as both a God of love and a God of humility.

Once we understand that love and humility are constant characteristics of the Creator of all things, we can readily understand why God chose the unpretentious young virgin Mary, of an obscure village, to quietly usher his Son into the world. Simply put, that's why he chose Mary. God is eternal, yes, but that's not the heart of God. The heart of God is love. Mary was "highly favored" undoubtedly because of her simple childlike love and trust in God. God is all-powerful, yes, but that too is not the heart of God. God's more significant aspect is his wondrous humility.

That humility startles me each Christmas as I ponder the surprising way Jesus comes to us, a little baby with tiny fingers and tiny toes, lying in a wooden food trough for animals, a manger lined with straw. Each year of my life, as I walk through Holy Week on my way to Good Friday and Easter, I am once again astonished at how God chose to redeem the world through his Son's unspectacular death on a cross. It was not unlike any of the other thousands of crucifixions of that period except, of course, in what it represented. Then his body was modestly buried in a borrowed tomb. How appropriate that such a God should choose a trusting teen who would respond to the angel Gabriel so simply, so humbly, "I am the Lord's servant. . . . May it be to me as you have said" (Luke 1:38).

We also see God's humility in the design of the universe. The sun is so huge and so hot that tongues of fire leap some ten thousand miles into space before retreating back into the seething surface with its unimaginable heat. You do not want to get too close to this fireball, which is the equivalent of more than 300,000 Earths in terms of its volume. Because of God's humility, he places this seething immensity ninety-three million miles from the Earth so that it is life-producing instead of dangerous or consuming. Moreover, the distance between the Earth and the sun remains so constant throughout a period of one thousand years that we have no reason to be afraid of the sun. It is one of the most stable and dependable forces in the universe. Without it, we would be unable to grow food. Without it, this little planet would turn to ice. Without it, the earth would exist in a permanent and unbearable darkness.

Or consider the planet Jupiter. It is so huge that it is twice as massive as all the other planets combined. You would need to line up eleven Earths side by side like bowling balls resting in their racks to equal Jupiter's imposing diameter of nearly eighty thousand miles. Or to put it another way, it would require more than three hundred Earths compressed together to form a sphere having the bulk of Jupiter! But because of God's humility, this gigantic planet is placed so far from the Earth that we scarcely know where to find it in the sky.

When we refer to God's humility, we are not suggesting that he is a God with lesser power. He is still the God of infinite power who has formed the stunning galaxies with their millions of stars. But they are all so remote to the Earth that they produce only wonder in us, not fear or panic. Jupiter is so stable in its orbit that we have no reason ever to fear it bringing destruction to our planet.

Our universe showcases God's power in terms of its colossal stars and staggering distances. It also depicts the humility of God, who chooses not to be in our face with his colossal creations. With the aid of telescopes and technology, we can sit in comfortable chairs to safely behold and explore the wonders of his creative mind and infinite power—wonders that he always places in the far reaches of space for our sense of security and physical safety. Their locations are consistently determined by a God who is thoroughly characterized by humility.

INTEGRATING

Now we come to the important task of applying what we have learned about humility to our marriages. If God the Father and God the Son are characterized by humility as much as love, just imagine the implications for us as beings who are trifling and small when set against the objects of his universe and the vastness of space. No wonder the ancient songwriter offers these lyrics in Psalm 8, "When I consider your heavens, the work of your fingers, the moon and the stars, which you have set in place, what is man that you are mindful of him, the son of man that you care for him?" (Ps. 8:3–4). The very proportions of creation seem to argue that humility is a must for every man and woman on the planet.

Therefore, it is not a question of whether we are to be humble or not. The real question is, how do we walk with humility? If God Almighty is clothed in humility, how could we ever excuse ourselves from striving for this virtue? How do we get down off our pedestals of pretension and live our lives fully convinced that we are not better than others? And if we are not better than others, are not our spouses included in those "others"? Just look at our scriptural focus for this chapter: "Do nothing out of selfish ambition or vain conceit, *but in humility consider others better than yourselves*. Each of you should look not only to your own interests, but also to the interests of others" (Phil. 2:3–4, emphasis mine).

I believe that it really is possible for you or me to "consider others better than ourselves." The Word does not say to consider most others better than ourselves. Nor does it say that we are to consider others better than ourselves most of the time. Either of those statements would be difficult enough to accomplish. However, we are commanded to "consider others better than yourselves." If that does not sound realistic or possible for you, take into account the accompanying command. "*Your attitude* should be the same as that of Christ Jesus: Who, being in very nature God, did not consider equality with God something to be grasped, *but made himself nothing*, taking the very nature of a servant, *being made in human likeness*" (Phil. 2:5–7, emphasis mine).

The author of Philippians is suggesting that if the eternal, all-knowing God chose to be "made in human likeness" and also to "make himself nothing," who on earth could be so arrogant as to think that such humility should not be expected of him or her? The psalmist is amazed that God even notices us since we are so infinitesimally small in contrast to the proportions of the universe.

"When I consider your heavens, the work of your fingers, the moon and the stars, which you have set in place, what is man that you are mindful of him?" (Ps. 8:3–4). Placed beside the stars of heaven, we are virtually at the vanishing point. We could easily be overlooked!

The Scriptures strongly urge us to clothe ourselves in humility so that we see our spouses as among those "others" who are to be regarded as "better than ourselves." Is that seriously doable? Rather than make up an imagined situation, I invite you to consider my life. I am a graduate of Princeton Theological Seminary, regarded by some as one of the best seminaries in the nation. It is my understanding that less than 1 percent of the earth's population has had the privilege of such higher education. So how am I to look at the unconscious man lying on the sidewalk, an empty liquor bottle just beyond his hand? A recovered alcoholic once said to me as a part of his personal testimony, "There, but for the grace of God, go I." That is to say, I was blessed with a wife who sacrificed for me, working alongside me full-time for eight years so I could have this privileged time of study. The man lying there on the cold pavement probably had no such wife. If I had been put through what he endured over many years, I may have ended up with much the same tragic outcome.

Again, consider how my parents raised me. Both my mom and dad were Christians who lived out their faith day by day. I cannot remember a time when my father punished me unfairly. Mom was always compassionate toward me—even on the day that I took my bike into the street, contrary to my parents' instructions, and ran it into a parked car! I know nothing of the family background of the man I passed by in the heart of Philadelphia who was too drunk to respond and I was too anxious to risk stopping. But if we were able to investigate his childhood, I would be surprised to find that he had parents like mine. I dare not act superior to him. In God's eyes he is surely my brother.

I was blessed with a mom and dad who cheered me on all through college and seminary. There were those moments when tears welled up in me, and I thought I could not make it. At that point, I had a wife who gave me a hug and told me she trusted me to give it my best, nothing more, nothing less. We prayed together. If that soul lying there unconscious on the pavement had experiences similar to mine, I would be astounded. Looking back to that day, I think God was as disappointed in my lack of courage to take that man in my arms and at least deliver him to a detox center where he could receive substantial help. God was undoubtedly pained by the unconscious man's desperate condition of homelessness and (most likely) hopelessness.

Or consider our marriage. Joanne and I did not have perfect parents, but we did have authentic Christian parents who let my sister and me know in tangible ways that they loved us and so did God. When we did something wrong, they never over-reacted in anger. Their punishments were fair and deserved. They sat us down and calmly talked with us. They looked us in the eyes to see if they could detect innocence or guilt. My parents never showed any favoritism toward my sister or me. When we were married, all four of our parents gave support to our marriage. My wife became as important to my parents as I was. Joanne was accepted into our family long before we were married. I was likewise welcomed into hers. All these blessings are some of the more notable reasons why I achieved whatever I accomplished.

Yet the derelict's story may be quite different. His father may have been verbally or sexually abusive, or both. His mother may have been on drugs or practicing prostitution, or both. His parents may have constantly favored another sibling while repeatedly telling him he was worthless. His life may have begun in the shadows of an unplanned pregnancy. He may have felt unwanted throughout his entire childhood.

I am not suggesting that God is powerless to redeem us from such things as a bad temper or the hurt caused by poor parenting or even the trauma of physical abuse. God is a transformer of men and women by the Holy Spirit's power. None of us needs to remain where we are, especially in terms of our marriages. Any among us can find new direction and hope in the life of Jesus Christ. But we need to beware of thinking we are better than another because of what we see on the surface. "Man looks on the outward appearance, but the LORD looks on the heart" (1 Sam. 16:7).

Try this simple exercise. Pretend you're the star witness in a court case that involves your wife or husband. You need to convince the court that your spouse is in fact "the better half." Could you make your presentation convincing to the judge and jury? Here is what I would say about my wife:

Honorable judge and jury, I ask you to recognize that my wife is decisively my better half. First of all, Joanne is a delight and joy to be with. Our friends love to visit us because a visit together is always a time of good humor, gentle teasing, joy, and laughter. Joanne always has on the tip of her tongue those delightful family stories that are fun to share. When we receive a thank-you note following an informal dinner get-together with six or seven of our friends, the most frequent line is, "We had such a great time!" or "It was so good to laugh again with friends!" We both cherish our friends, but I tend to be serious for the most part. Joanne, however, will lighten and brighten any gathering of which she's a part.

Joanne is also extremely capable with multitasking. While I am still jotting down the things I hope to get done during the coming week, she is already taking the initiative to weed the flower gardens or check on the outcome of a friend's outpatient tests. While I am still thinking about how to most effectively deal with a problem, Joanne is already on the phone asking specific questions about errors on a medical bill, or getting a free estimate on a tree removal. She can find the phone number needed to solve any kind of problem in a fraction of the time I would require. These skills are so well developed that when I share with her a particular need or problem (such as getting our chimney cleaned or troubleshooting a mysterious leak in our basement), I at times find myself thinking afterwards, *By mid-morning, she will have the answer, or at the very least know what our options are.* Joanne is a remarkable problem solver! As for me, I am at the hardware store picking up a replacement light switch.

Joanne is also a giver, far more than I am. She uses the phone daily to keep in touch with family and friends, especially when there is a health problem, unemployment, depression, loneliness, etc. She simply loves people! She is ready to get together with friends tomorrow night or early next week, whereas in many cases I would prefer to set a date in the next month.

My wife is also an initiator. She will always be the first to realize that the rhododendron needs to be pruned, ants are gathering behind the garage, or the pillows in the master bedroom need to be replaced. And she will normally be the one to set an appointment to have the carpets cleaned, or to set a day to help our granddaughters shop for back-to-school supplies and outfits. The same is true when we consider overnighters and vacations. Joanne gets on the phone and after a burst of calls involving most of our states, she has confirmed reservations in the most elegant setting and at an unbeatable price. I would prefer to wait until next week, after I have completed several more things on my checklist, and especially the installation of the light switch!

Honorable judge and jury, you have here what borders on being a no-brainer. To sum up, my wife is in countless ways a greater blessing to me than I have ever been to her. Please be assured that I am still trying my best and eagerly learning each day how to be a partner who is a worthy match."

You may want to give this a try. Your personal observations, if honestly identified, should turn up some significant discoveries!

A Prayer

Lord Jesus, I am sure of one thing: that no one ever walked this earth with the fullness of humility you embodied throughout your earthly life. Help me also to walk humbly in your presence, and to embody this beautiful attitude that considers others as better than oneself. Forgive my own tendencies, however subtle, to regard myself as better than the helpmate you have given me. Because I do not change very easily, please be patient with me as I make a deliberate effort to embrace the attitude I see in your life, making yourself as nothing, "taking the very nature of a servant." Grant me the humility that was characteristic of Mary, who gave herself so obediently to your plan. This coming week help me to be more aware of my wife's/husband's special qualities that caused me to love her/him in the first place. And especially help me to turn my eyes away from other people's faults, and to spend my time with you amending my own. In your great love and power I pray. Amen.

Three Questions

1. Identify two significant ways in which your wife (husband) exceeds your own capacities, causing you to admire her (him).

2. Richard C. Halverson has said, "It is hard for a 'superior' person to be used of the Lord." Why do you suppose that a marriage is less fulfilling and less intimate when one partner (or both) sees himself/herself as "superior" to the other?

3. What are some of the evidences you could cite to support the thesis of this chapter, that "humility is a constant in the life of Jesus. Never does he step outside of this spiritual trait"?

INSIGHTS

I have never accepted what many people have kindly said, namely that I inspired the nation. It was the nation and the race dwelling all around the globe that had the lion heart. I had the luck to be called upon to give the roar.

—Winston Churchill

I believe the first test of a truly great man is his humility.

—John Ruskin

And what does the LORD require of you? To act justly and to love mercy and to walk humbly with your God.

—Mic. 6:8

I used to think that God's gifts were on shelves one above the other, and that the taller we grew in Christian character the more easily we could reach them. I now find that God's gifts are on shelves one beneath the other, and that it is not a question of growing taller but of stooping down, to get his best gifts.

—F. B. Meyer

Oh, beware! Do not seek to be something! Let me be nothing, and Christ be all in all.

—John Wesley (in a letter to Francis Asbury)

Live in harmony with one another. Do not be proud, but be willing to associate with people of low position. Do not be conceited.

—Rom. 12:16

The true way to be humble is not to stoop until you are smaller than yourself, but to stand at your real height against some higher nature that will show you what the real smallness of your greatness is.

—Phillips Brooks

Someone asked one of the ancient Fathers how he might obtain true humility, and he answered, "By keeping your eyes off other people's faults, and fixing them on your own."

—Alphonse Rodriguez

In Christian service the branches that bear the most fruit hang the lowest.

—Unknown

CHAPTER TWELVE

When Jesus reached the spot, he looked up and said to him, "Zacchaeus, come down immediately. I must stay at your house today." So he came down at once and welcomed him gladly.

—Luke 19:5–6

Reaching for the Best: The Graciousness of Christ

INTERPERSONAL

Joanne and I had been married for three years when I felt the call to pastoral ministry. Joanne shared in my sense of call and was as enthusiastic as I was about the challenging adventure ahead of us: seven years of full-time higher education to be ordained for Christian ministry. We sold our Cape Cod home in suburban Baltimore and began studies at Westminster College in New Wilmington, Pennsylvania. When we shared our calling with our pastor, he listened carefully and then advised us not to try it because we were now married with new responsibilities and expectations and the prospect of a family. Although we were let down by his response, we never thought of backing down. In fact, I think we became more determined to make it work!

I did very well with all of the tests during my first semester at Westminster, but then final exams came. I could not believe how much material I had to review for my five classes. The tests occurred within a four-day period, with two of them back-to-back on the same day. I had been out of school for three years and was apprehensive about my capacity to step back into full-time studies. This would be a totally new experience for me and for our families. Neither of our families had ever produced a college graduate. Because of family circumstances, my mom had to settle for a ninth-grade education. My dad completed high school and worked as a bookkeeper in a small company. No one in my family could coach me about how to prepare for college-level finals.

The night before my back-to-back finals, I was reviewing my notes late into the night. The more I studied, the more I felt overwhelmed by the sheer volume of information and concepts that could be on the exams. One of my courses the following day was physics, a required course that I felt had nothing to do with a pastor's work. My physics test grades throughout the semester were among my lowest grades.

All I could think of was a key remark made by the president of the college at the convocation service at the beginning of the year. "Look at the person sitting to your left and the person to your right. One of those two students will not be here on campus for the sophomore year." I was certain that the missing student would be me! *It just is not possible for me to remember all this stuff,* I thought, and tears started coursing down my face.

At that moment, my wife stepped into the room to see if I needed a cup of coffee and immediately saw my tears. She came over, sat on the arm of the chair, and put her arm around me, her head touching mine. For a long while I could not say a thing. It really did not matter. Joanne knew that I was feeling overwhelmed. Finally, I choked, "I just can't do this!" Although I do not recall all that she said to support and encourage me, the one thing I remember is that she trusted me. She said that we had to trust the outcome to the Lord. "All he expects of you is that you do your best." Her arm was still around me. We had a cup of hot chocolate, and I was ready to tackle my notes for a few more hours.

As I look back at that experience more than forty years ago, I am amazed by how gracious my wife was with me. While I was a college student, she was working full-time as a comptometer operator for the local telephone company so we could pay tuition bills, our apartment rent, and our other expenses. It was a sacrifice for her as much as it was for me. Many nights we had little time together because of my studies. She could have easily said to me that night, "Look, Bob, I've worked for the past six months to pay the bills. The least you can do is to get decent grades." Or she could have said, "I can't believe you! If you mess up on this, I will feel so embarrassed to have to go back home and face our family and friends."

At the time she was only twenty-three, but she had the maturity and faith to know how to encourage me. Joanne's graciousness and confidence in me were a real comfort. And with that encouragement, I plowed through the rest of my finals. My grades were not all A's, but I would graduate *cum laude* four years later.

Would any of your friends describe you as gracious? Does your spouse see you as a gracious partner?

INSPIRING

In the days when the judges ruled, there was a famine in the land, and a man from Bethlehem in Judah, together with his wife and two sons, went to live for a while in the country of Moab. The man's name was Elimelech, his wife's name Naomi, and the names of his two sons were Mahlon and Kilion. They were Ephrathites from Bethlehem, Judah. And they went to Moab and lived there.

Now Elimelech, Naomi's husband, died, and she was left with her two sons. They married Moabite women, one named Orpah and the other Ruth. After they had lived there about ten years, both Mahlon and Kilion also died, and Naomi was left without her two sons and her husband.

When she heard in Moab that the LORD had come to the aid of his people by providing food for them, Naomi and her daughters-in-law prepared to return home from there. With her two daughters-in-law she left the place where she had been living and set out on the road that would take them back to the land of Judah.

Then Naomi said to her two daughters-in-law, "Go back, each of you, to your mother's home. May the LORD show kindness to you, as you have shown to your dead and to me. May the LORD grant that each of you will find rest in the home of another husband."

Then she kissed them and they wept aloud and said to her, "We will go back with you to your people."

But Naomi said, "Return home, my daughters. Why would you come with me? Am I going to have any more sons, who could become your husbands? Return home, my daughters; I am too old to have another husband. Even if I thought there was still hope for me—even if I had a husband tonight and then gave birth to sons—would you wait until they grew up? Would you remain unmarried for them? No, my daughters. It is more bitter for me than for you, because the LORD's hand has gone out against me!"

At this they wept again. Then Orpah kissed her mother-in-law good-by, but Ruth clung to her.

"Look," said Naomi, "your sister-in-law is going back to her people and her gods. Go back with her."

But Ruth replied, "Don't urge me to leave you or to turn back from you. Where you go I will go, and where you stay I will stay. Your people will be my people and your God my God. Where you die I will die, and there I will be buried. May the LORD deal with me, be it ever so severely, if anything but death separates you and me." When Naomi realized that Ruth was determined to go with her, she stopped urging her.

—Ruth 1:1–18

IMAGING

Naomi thought that she would always live in Bethlehem. It was a very small town—really, just a hamlet. Yet she loved it there. She had been born in Bethlehem and knew everyone. It was like growing up in a large family. She was happily married some twenty years now (where had the time gone!), and God had blessed Elimelech and her with two strong, healthy sons, Mahlon and Kilion. When she wasn't busy preparing meals for her three men, or washing their work clothes, or tending her modest garden, she found pleasure in decorating their small but well-built home with roses from Sharon, or with lilies she had found growing wild alongside the road—carrying them home in her arms protectively like a precious gift.

Then came the harsh years of famine. The earth that had so faithfully sustained their lives year after year now became a lifeless dust—at times blown about by the wind, and endlessly tortured by the unremitting heat of the blistering Palestinian sun. Naomi's family barely survived the next two years. Finally surrendering to the drought's relentlessness, they finally did what some of their neighbors had already done. They abandoned their home to live outside the large region distressed by the drought. For Ruth and Elimelech and their sons—now young men—it meant moving at least thirty miles away to Moab, a foreign nation with a strange language and even stranger religious customs and beliefs. The family missed the familiarity and simplicity of Bethlehem and unenthusiastically began the difficult but necessary task of earning the respect of the Moabites and understanding their perplexing and at times repulsive religious rites.

Naomi tried to be strong in this new and often hostile environment. Her warmth and natural gentleness, coupled with her unique sense of humor, caused her to be liked by virtually all of her neighbors—especially when it was learned that her handsome sons were eligible for marriage. But their new and demanding life was so stressful that it took Elimelech's life within a year. Naomi was overcome with grief. She tried to be grateful for the blessing afforded her in having two sons who were very loving, constantly assuring her of their support and protection. But the loss of her homeland, followed so closely by the loss of her husband, had caused her to struggle with how a loving God could allow all this to happen. Her grief became so agonizing and all-consuming that it seemed to transform her personality—drawing her joyous, self-giving spirit into the grayness of self-doubt, with a seemingly endless chain of unanswerable questions.

During this heart-wrenching struggle, the inevitable happened: her two adventuresome sons fell in love with two beautiful Moabite women. The two brothers found an unquenchable joy in their romantic pursuits, perhaps because their most recent years had been filled with so much hardship and misfortune. Their high-spirited courtships—catalyzed by their newfound joys and a mutual celebration of their good fortune—quickly drew both brothers into marriage. Mahlon married Orpah in a religious ceremony that seemed to Naomi to be more Moabite than Israelite. Kilion did somewhat better at being more faithful to his religious heritage when he married Ruth, but it was still without the warmth and familiarity of their lovely synagogue and dear friends back in Bethlehem. These changes further burdened Naomi because she saw even less of her sons now that their attention was focused on their marriages and the attendant array of responsibilities.

Then came the heaviest blow of all. After living in Moab for just a decade, both of Naomi's sons tragically died. Ironically, their deaths occurred just a few months apart. By this time, Naomi had become so close to Orpah and Ruth that she could no longer think of them as daughters-in-law. They were her dear and delightful daughters. The common experience of the three women, while tragic, seemed to solidify their relationship. Naomi felt confident that she and her daughters would always be inseparable. And yet, without the men, she knew that it would be a difficult life of impoverishment—unless they remarried.

Naomi seemed to have more trouble working through her grief than Ruth and Orpah, perhaps because she had been married longer. She was also older and lacked the resilience of youth. She prayed daily that God would provide some way for her to break free of her oppressive feelings of grief and loss. Her many tearful prayers seemed to be answered when a caravan of Israelites traveling through Moab brought news that the years of famine in Judah had ended. Judah's cities and towns were gradually being repopulated, and farming was once again productive. Naomi longed to reunite with her extended family back home even though she had no idea how many of her kinfolk had returned to Bethlehem. She took immediate steps to go home. She knew that Ruth and Orpah would understand.

The news, once announced, did not really astonish the girls. They had often heard Naomi talk about her life in Bethlehem and her family and friends there. They loved to hear her talk about her belief in a God who loved his people. There was something out of the ordinary about her life, especially the unimaginable uniqueness of her gracious and forgiving God. They were intrigued by her life and could understand why she would want to return home.

For their part, Orpah and Ruth wanted so very much to keep their cherished relationship with Naomi. With little discussion or hesitation, they decided not only to accompany Naomi to her homeland, but also to live with her indefinitely in Bethlehem or wherever she resettled. After all, the three had always found considerable comfort and joy in one another. Together they could rebuild their shattered lives, and, hopefully, find a new beginning in their new surroundings.

Their decision gave Naomi considerable joy. She was thrilled to know that both of her sons' wives expressed such a strong desire to remain at her side. It also comforted her to know that she would be returning to Bethlehem accompanied by two loving women who were such a substantial and joyous part of her sons' lives and were significant to her as well.

Together the three women prepared to set out for Bethlehem, for the most part seeing their relocation as an exciting venture. Ruth and Orpah would share in a completely new way of life. Their departure from Moab was not without tears; but once made, their decision was resolute and unwavering. They saw it as a personal adventure involving only a minimum of risk. All three women confidently anticipated happier years ahead.

However, our deepest feelings sometimes surprise us with an unexpected change of heart. As they traveled toward Bethlehem, Naomi felt increasingly troubled about what they had decided to do. She felt a new and growing concern welling up inside her. She was taking these two lovely women away from their families and everything familiar to them. She remembered how difficult her own loss of Elimelech had been, and Orpah and Ruth had experienced that same traumatic loss even earlier in their marriages. Neither had known the joys of childbirth and mothering. Their decision to leave Moab to be with Naomi involved considerable sacrifice.

The only right thing to do was to send them back to their homeland and families. And since the three women had been traveling with a caravan, Naomi felt assured that her own safety and the safety of the girls would not be compromised if the two of them traveled back to their homes the same way. She would therefore insist they return to their families, who were surely going through their own time of anguish and loss. Their families had courageously said their farewells without knowing if they would ever see their daughters again.

It took all of the resolve and courage Naomi could muster, but when the caravan stopped to rest at midday, Naomi did what she knew she had to do. As soon as the animals had been cared for, she put her arms around Ruth and Orpah and said frankly, "My daughters, you have been a great comfort to me, but it is important to me that you now return to your homes." She paused to regain control of her voice. And then, feeling confident that she was doing what God wanted her to do, she gave them her sincere blessing. "And may the Lord show kindness to you, as you have shown kindness to your husbands and to me." She was feeling more composed, thinking of their joy and the joy of their families as she continued. "Now go, and may the Lord be pleased to give both of you happiness and peace in the rich life of another loving husband!" Having said it, Naomi was confident they would readily see how appropriate were her concerns. They would surely respond with warm hugs and begin to make their plans to return home. It seemed so clear to Naomi at that moment that it was not right their lives should be so restricted of blessings to comfort an old woman who had failed to trust God as fully as she could.

When Orpah showed signs of listening to Naomi's advice, though not without tears and affection, Naomi felt even more conviction that her intuition was right. Naomi felt a surge of gladness in her heart. She had found the courage to give back to the two women their essential freedom and, more than that, their lives! Her joy in restoring such a precious gift reminded her of past joys when she had more carefully followed the Lord's will, no matter how difficult. Her tears were a strange mixture of sadness in parting and the deep satisfaction of doing what she felt God had whispered in her heart. Smiling despite the tears coursing down her cheeks, she again said as warmly and as lightly as she could, "Return home, my dear daughters! After all, I do not have any more sons who could be your husbands!" She continued almost teasingly, determined to keep it light. "Even if I remarried and was blessed with sons similar to Mahlon and Kilion, would you want to sit around for decades waiting until they grew up?" Glancing at both of them, she said with a more serious, lowered voice, "No, my daughters, please return home!"

Naomi felt good about how it had all come out. She saw confirmed in Orpah's eyes a corresponding discovery that this was what they needed to do, however difficult it was at that moment. These two women, Naomi and Orpah, seemed to understand and accept a sudden discovery. They had shared in a wonderful relationship for years, yet the hour had come to say good-by. Naomi felt convinced that God in his mercy had given her the words to say and had helped her to offer them humbly and graciously.

After Orpah had embraced Naomi for a long while, she stepped back to allow Ruth to do the same. Ruth stepped forward quietly to embrace Naomi, not as a warm farewell, but more like a child who could not be consoled. Ruth buried her head in the folds of Naomi's robe, holding her tightly, not knowing what to say. Naomi could not see Ruth's face, yet she knew that something quite different was being experienced in her heart. When Ruth's sobbing had subsided, she found words to share—words that were broken by sobs and difficult to hear—still buried as she was in the loose folds of Naomi's robe.

Her thoughts came like pieces of leftover fabric that had to be pieced together. "Please do not encourage me . . . to leave you . . . or to change my mind about going with you." Her words came out slowly and painfully between anguished sobs. Naomi's heart was about to break as Ruth continued to struggle to find the right words. "Wherever you go, I will go . . . wherever you live . . . I will live . . . your people will be my people . . . and your God my God . . . Wherever you die, I will also die." And then came a long quietness. Finally, she lifted her head from the comfort of the folds of clothing to look pleadingly into Naomi's eyes, now declaring with a surprising strength, "And may the Lord deal with me severely if he has to—if anything but death separates you and me!"

Naomi's heart melted upon hearing Ruth's tearfully passionate words. She had expected nothing like this. In her own heart she had decisively set the two girls free, only to discover that one of them did not want that kind of freedom. Ruth wanted to be free to make her own choices, and her choice was to remain with Naomi. Ruth's surprising response required of Naomi an even deeper graciousness— a graciousness that even offered the freedom to come alongside her, the freedom to choose a life that might include poverty and pain. What if her choice proved to be unwise, and she actually had far fewer opportunities to know happiness again? What if her choice was simply the choice of a life of deprivation and sacrifice? Naomi now realized how much she loved them both. Whether they came with her or returned home was their choice to make. Her responsibility was to accept and support their decisions, and to assure them of her gracious and unconditional love.

INTERPRETING

Naomi's graciousness toward Orpah and Ruth seems somewhat late coming, does it not? How many miles from Moab were the three women when Naomi finally saw the light—to let them go and build a life of their own? And yet, in Naomi's defense, occasions of expressed graciousness do not pepper most of our lives. If we are honest, our expressions of graciousness—if and when they occur— are often slow in becoming a reality. Most of us struggle as Naomi did to think and act graciously toward those who are closest to us. Naomi's daughters-in-law had captivated the hearts of her two sons and they had married them. They had become a close family. How gracious are we with those family members who comprise our most primary relationships—our spouses, our children, our parents?

What do you suppose was happening to Naomi as she began to pack up her belongings and return to little Bethlehem, which she undoubtedly still thought of as her hometown? She was probably finding it difficult to say farewell to the two girls with whom she had forged such a strong bond. All three had lost a loving and faithful mate and were coping with one of the toughest transitions required of us.

This traumatic human experience had bonded these women into an inseparable trio. They had cried together on many occasions and found encouragement in one another's embraces. Their common ground of intense personal pain and grief had united them. It would not have readily occurred to any of the women that other considerations could be so significant as to influence their decision to go their separate ways.

That is why it took hours, or possibly even days, of travel in the hot sun for Naomi to see what she was doing to these two young women who had their whole lives yet before them. Perhaps it was the step-by-step distancing of herself and the girls from Moab that brought about the clarity of her discovery. She came to see that she was, in a sense, robbing from their lives to enrich her own. Naomi's emotional dependence on these two loving women ultimately had the effect of restricting and entrapping them. With that important insight came both the courage and the motivation to set them free of her own needs.

So we can at least rejoice that Naomi saw her own selfishness—however subtle—and acted with a spirit of selflessness and graciousness to release these two daughters whom she so much loved. To her credit, she did so without seeming to be the martyr, e.g., "I do not know how I will ever manage on my own." Nor did Naomi convey her feelings with a sense of exaggerated guilt, e.g., "I cannot believe how long I have held on to you both, blind to my own selfishness." Such expressions would have gone too far, since the "blindness" had largely been caused by the emotional turmoil of their common grief. Up to this point, all three had desperately needed one another to work through their grief and to find comfort. Now the time had come for them to move on from their paralyzing grief. Naomi is to be commended for her spiritual insight. Had she not acted so considerately to return these daughters to their families and set them free, they might have eventually come to resent Naomi for limiting their future possibilities.

In the light of the biblical narrative, let us now make an attempt at defining graciousness. When I experience another person's graciousness toward me, what am I actually receiving? Is it not the freedom and confidence to make my own decisions, knowing that they will be respected? Does it not involve another's trust in me to walk in my God-given freedom while also remaining absolutely true to my own beliefs and values, true to my relationship with God, and true to myself? Is it not discovering that the other person loves me deeply—and will always love me—but without any hold on me, without any obligation, without any attempt to control me?

Christlike graciousness is also an expression of confidence that the other person will do what is right, what is God's will, and therefore what is best for both persons. Graciousness has to do with an awareness that every person is to be treated as a child of God—that every person is as significant to God as I am, and therefore must be set free of every demand and dependency. Otherwise, how could a person faithfully fulfill God's plan for his life? Graciousness involves untangling oneself from every tendency or temptation to claim, control, or consume another person's life for our own benefit.

Some years ago I participated in a weekly prayer group with five other pastors. We spent two hours each week sharing our ministries, highlighting our joys, confessing our failures, working through our frustrations, and praying for one another. One week I came to the prayer group feeling discouraged. I could not get my congregation to grow in terms of the attendance of the worshipping body on any given Sunday. This stagnation in growth had gone on for about two years and was causing me mounting frustration. I was taking some seminars on preaching at Princeton Theological Seminary and elsewhere. I hoped that I could be retrained to preach more effectively to this generation. When I completed a seminar, it was not easy for me to leave the comfort of the pulpit and speak more conversationally from the floor of the sanctuary, as the seminar had encouraged us to do. I prayed my way through these major changes (at least they were major to me!), but worship attendance remained unchanged. All this I shared with the group. When our time together was ending, we had our usual time of prayer. And this is what I remember of one of the prayers offered by a pastor/friend:

> Dear God, we want to thank you for our brother Bob, and for his
> pastor's heart. We praise you that he loves his people and wants

them to have the very best that Jesus has to offer—both for him and for his congregation. Help him to understand that faithful preaching does not always mean a growing church. Father, we rejoice that even as he faces health issues and retirement issues, he is eagerly pursuing new ways to preach your Word. Receive our deep gratitude and joy that Bob is unwilling to coast through these final years of ministry—as some do—but rather has chosen to sprint as it were to the finish line of his full-time Christian service. In Jesus' precious name! Amen.

What an encouragement that prayer was to me! The person who prayed it trusted me to give my very best, and saw my attempts at learning new methods of preaching as a means of remaining dedicated to pastoral ministry. He saw me in the best possible light—not as a frustrated preacher, but as a man "sprinting to the finish line." As I drove back to my office that morning, I felt more exhilaration and inspiration than I had felt for many months. I was released from my frustrated struggle to change worship attendance. The gracious words of a person who loved me and fully trusted me to do my ministry with integrity, excellence, and imagination had made a remarkable difference in my self-perception, outlook, and attitude.

We see graciousness at its best in the life of Christ. Consider Jesus' personal concern for a woman who had just barely touched, for a second or so, the hem of his robe as he was pushed along by the press of a crowd that had become too enthusiastic, even unruly. (See Matthew 9:20–22 for the entire narrative.) Women of every culture have for centuries been sensitive to that time in their monthly cycle that has required everything from isolation to protection. This woman, however, had a problem that perpetually pursued her—a hemorrhaging for many years. All manner of medical expertise could not resolve her problem and she remained anguished by the unwanted side effects of such a disorder. She had been very nearly ostracized by the community, who would not accept the conditions and plight of her "illness." Yet, despite the almost delirious excitement of the crowd and the forward thrusting of this throng of people, Jesus pulls the whole mass to a dead halt to find the person who had so lightly touched his robe for just a second or so. Compassionately, he speaks with her to discover her need, and then graciously gives her the longing of her heart—the complete healing of the hemorrhaging. The marvelous graciousness of Jesus!

INTEGRATING

When our granddaughter Syd was six years old, we were leaving a restaurant that gave each child a helium balloon. Syd was delighted because hers was yellow—her favorite color. As we were getting into the van, Joanne was concerned that the balloon might be accidentally lost because Syd had other things in her hands. Syd was willing to turn the balloon over to grandma, and then moved to her car seat. In the process the balloon went free and quickly climbed skyward, lifted on a breeze. Grandma was really upset with herself for losing Syd's trophy. "Oh, Syd, I just lost your balloon . . . *I am so sorry!*" Syd turned around and looking at her grandma, said without a tear, "It's okay, Grandma . . . let's laugh about it!" Instead of tears, Charis and Syd both wanted to watch the balloon to see how long they could see it traveling to the clouds. It got smaller and smaller, then finally disappeared from our sight. What a delightful experience of a child's graciousness despite her own loss.

I have often thought about Syd's very gracious words, "It's okay, Grandma . . . let's laugh about it!" Thereafter, when we would drop a fresh egg on the kitchen floor, or arrive at our front door in an unexpected downpour while searching for the right key, one of us would quip, "It's okay . . . let's laugh about it!"

How do you and your spouse handle setbacks and sufferings? If you find that you can still enjoy life and remain cheerful despite your setbacks, you can close this book! Most of us need a lot of hugs, a lot of friends who can listen to our pain, as well as persons who will come alongside us with practical help, like dropping off a pot of homemade soup or picking up our kids at school and taking them to soccer practice.

Here is one of the big reasons why God gathered us into the fellowship of the church. Jesus did not want us to have to face our most difficult days alone. "Praise be to the God and Father of our

Lord Jesus Christ, the Father of compassion and the God of all comfort, who comforts us in all our troubles, *so that we can comfort those in any trouble with the comfort we ourselves have received from God*" (2 Cor. 1:3–4, emphasis mine). God has given us the church, not because he wants to see a cathedral on every other corner and crossroads, but because he wants us together as family, as community, as a circle of caring, connected by his love.

When we experience a gracious person, it is so refreshing and affirming. It is like a breath of fresh air! I am fortunate to have several gracious friends. They trust me to be true to my faith in Jesus Christ. They begin with the assumption that I am giving my best and striving for excellence. They are gentle souls who have a remarkable sensitivity to everyone they meet. They consistently and continually refrain from all negativism and criticism, all sarcasm and suspicion, all argument and arrogance, all put-downs and pessimism. Such persons bear in their lives a noticeable joyfulness, a genuine humility, and an ease of affirming those around them and expressing gratefulness—beginning with their spouses. If only we would strive to bear such graciousness every day in terms of how we connect with our mates.

When our daughter died, her husband, Dave, invited four of her girlfriends to be part of the memorial service by offering their personal thoughts about their friendship with "San" and how they saw her. Their experiences with Sandy were different in expression, but in every case the remarks of these four women were marked with a lovely graciousness. Sandy is my daughter and so I have a distinct bias in the way I perceive her! Nevertheless, she had a few liabilities like all of us. Note, however, the way her friend Tammy Getty so lovingly and graciously spoke of her:

> Sandy and I have been friends for twenty-seven years. We were the kind of friends that would sleep at one of our houses, staying up and talking all night long, only to go home and talk to each other on the phone for two more hours. We were teenage girls: sleepovers; ski trips; making milkshakes; beach trips; double dates; lots of letters; long phone conversations; walking in the snow;

taking college classes together; long phone conversations; college visits to each other; expanding our individual world of friends; meeting at the track to exercise; careers; weddings and husbands; baby showers and children; more long phone conversations; confronting a life-threatening illness; and now . . . death. How many of us are so blessed to say that we have been part of a friendship of such depths? For this I am so very thankful.

Sandy and I have shared love, laughter, sorrow, tears, joy, sadness, comfort, true happiness, and fear in our friendship. We have felt possibly every emotion that two friends could encounter, at times so thankful for each other, at other moments wanting to give up on each other. But through it all, San never gave up on me as a friend. And this was one of the most beautiful qualities that Sandy possessed—her ability to do something to the utmost, including nurturing a friendship, to give her all to things, to not do anything halfheartedly.

I have so many touching stories to share about San. But there is one that sticks so vividly in my mind. It was about three years ago, and I had just given birth to my fourth baby. By this time I was sure San had to be sick of making meals for me, but there she was, on my doorstep with dinner. I opened the door, in my pajamas, house a mess, kids running all over the place, and in she walks with this beautifully organized feast. She's got everything—homemade stuffed shells, Italian bread, salad dressing, ice cream for dessert, and the most intricately put together salad one could ever imagine. She has a big bowl of lettuce and all of the individual toppings, carefully sliced/diced/chopped or whatever, in individual zip-lock bags. There are cucumbers, croutons, peppers, tomatoes, and even cranberries, all lovingly prepared for our salad. I remember just standing there and considering the fact that it must have taken her all day to prepare this meal for us and wondering what she was going to have for dinner. But that was San. Her kitchen was probably a mess, I am sure her own family wasn't eating as lavishly that night, but her friend was being treated so specially. That was Sandy.

One last anecdote. For my most recent birthday, Sandy wanted to buy me a new Bible. She had just the right thing in mind, but of course wanted my input. So, as San frequently did, she'd call me to discuss it, and then call back to re-discuss it and find out if I really wanted this feature, or did I prefer another one. What size did I want? Should it go in my pocketbook or briefcase? Did I want leather, or a particular color? What translation did I like? So after much consultation throughout various conversations, she decided upon just the right Bible for me.

We had dinner out, just weeks ago, and she gave me the Bible. And, of course, there was a sweet and heartfelt inscription inside it. When I got home that night I could just picture Sandy, contemplating the right words to give to her friend to cherish this gift forever. She probably thought about it, wrote some ideas, rewrote other versions, and then finally settled on the words that would remain with me forever—that I would treasure always. She put her everything into what many of us see as a simple birthday present, or everyday meal, but to her was a true gift to a friend from one's heart. This was the way Sandy lived her life—with such focus and purpose about the things she deemed important.

Sandy was a true and faithful friend. I am at such a loss in contemplating her departure from my life. I find peace in knowing that she is at peace. And I thank God every day for the times I had with her."[11]

The other three testimonials by Sandy's dear friends were also thoughtful reflections graciously offered. Their showering of treasured memories helped Joanne and me to see Sandy's life in its greater fullness and richness. We were both comforted and strengthened. Our words can have so much power when they begin to approach the graciousness of Christ.

A Prayer

Dear Lord, thanks for your "lifetime" here on earth so I could see vividly what graciousness looks like as you related to persons like Naomi, Zacchaeus, and the woman who touched the hem of your robe. With your help and guidance, I desire to conduct my own life with the imprint of your graciousness—especially in my relationship with my mate. Set me free of my long-standing habits of subtle sarcasm, arrogant arguments, and hurtful put-downs. Fill my heart with an overflowing of your love, and grant to me a greater generosity in terms of my words of affirmation and gratitude. Day by day help me to bear more vividly the image of my Lord and his graciousness. In Jesus' precious name. Amen.

Three Questions

1. If you really desired to be more gracious toward your husband/wife, what single habit or failing in yourself would you concentrate on as your number one priority, so as to express the graciousness of Christ in your marriage?

2. Who within your family or among your friends could serve as a strong role model for graciousness? When you are with that person, pay attention to how he/she relates to others, so as to learn from him/her. If you do not see someone among your family and friends with this extraordinary quality, you might choose a celebrity such as Billy Graham, Michael Fox, or Oprah Winfrey.

3. Why do you suppose that many persons are unable to get motivated about learning how to live out a Christlike graciousness with their partners?

Insights

Grace is not sought nor bought nor wrought. It is a free gift of Almighty God to needy mankind.

—Billy Graham

Christ is no Moses, no exactor, no giver of laws, but a giver of grace, a Savior; he is infinite mercy and goodness, freely and bountifully giving to us.

—Martin Luther

We loved you so much that we were delighted to share with you not only the gospel of God but our lives as well, because you had become so dear to us.

—1 Thess. 2:8

May I only say that the fullest, deepest breath you will ever take, you will take when you come to understand at last that you are rid of more of the burden you have been to yourself than you had ever dreamed was possible.

—Paul Scherer

The greatest part of our happiness or misery depends on our dispositions and not on our circumstances.

—Martha Washington

Not how, so much, but that he should have come at all, is miracle, given the welcome to be expected at inns not starred for hospitality. Still, he came . . .

—David W. Romig

ENDNOTES

1. Used with permission of Anne B. Snow
2. Used with permission of composer John Ylvisaker. Copyright 1985. Box 321, Waverly, Iowa 50677. Reproduced from The Presbyterian Hymnal: Hymns, Psalms, and Spiritual Songs. Copyright 1990 Westminster John Knox Press.
3. Shared with the permission of Joseph Eby
4. See *The New Testament in Modern English* by J. B. Phillips, Revised Edition
5. Personal reference used with the permission of both Lydia Fehr and Bart Richwine
6. Shared with the gracious permission of Tom and Nancy Kitzmiller—two marvelous friends, encouragers, and a continuing source of incalculable joy
7. Personal reference used with her permission. Susan Caler is a dedicated educator who has ably served as Administrator of Valley Christian School in Huntingdon Valley, Pennsylvania, for over twelve years. She maintains an incredible balance between being a serious educator (she is a *cum laude* graduate of Geneva College and earned her Master of Education degree with Distinction at Arcadia University) and maintaining a personal interest in her students—she loves to get acquainted with her

students through conversations in the hallways, or taking two or three to shop at the mall, or visiting in their homes when there are acute family needs.

8. Personal reference used with her permission. Suzanne Dougherty is a much loved teacher by her third graders, and is highly qualified with Bachelor of Science degrees in Bible, Elementary Education, and Early Childhood Education. She has taught at Valley Christian School for over eight years.

9. Shared with the permission of Henry Nixon

10. Sharing in this major effort with the Kitzmillers has been one of the most meaningful experiences in giving and enabling others who are among the world's poorest families. Shared with permission.

11. Tamara Southerling Getty, affectionately known as "Tammy," is a dear friend of our family.